Popular Complete Smart Series

• Advanced •
Complete
MathSmart®
Grade 4

Credits

Photos (Back Cover "girl on left"/123RF.com, "boy" Jose Manuel Gelpi Diaz/123RF.com, "girl in middle"/123RF.com, "girl on right" Paul Hakimata/123RF.com, "memo board" Sandra Van Der Steen/123RF.com)

 Proud Sponsor of the Math Team of Canada 2017

Copyright © 2017 Popular Book Company (Canada) Limited

Printed in China

ISBN: 978-1-77149-202-7

ISBN: 978-1-77149-202-7

A Message to Parents

Advanced Complete MathSmart is an extension of our bestselling *Complete MathSmart* series. This series focuses on challenging word problems that require the application of the math concepts and skills that children have learned in the *Complete MathSmart* series.

The two sections in this book are designed to gradually develop your child's problem-solving and critical-thinking skills. In Section 1, each unit covers one core topic and begins with basic skills questions, followed by problem-solving questions that increase in difficulty as the unit progresses. It reinforces your child's math concepts and skills in the topic in focus. Working through this section, your child should be able to proficiently explain and illustrate the solutions to the word problems.

Section 2 provides abundant critical-thinking questions, each combining multiple topics from Section 1. The topics are integrated in different ways to provide a wide range of complex and challenging questions that help stimulate your child's mathematical reasoning and develop his or her critical-thinking skills.

An answer key with step-by-step solutions is also provided at the end of this comprehensive book. All the solutions are presented in a clear and organized way to allow your child to have a thorough understanding of the math concepts.

Advanced Complete MathSmart will not only improve your child's core math understanding and skills, but also develop his or her critical-thinking skills which are essential in solving daily life challenges.

Your Partner in Education,
Popular Book Co. (Canada) Ltd.

ISBN: 978-1-77149-202-7

Advanced Complete MathSmart®

Section 1:
Basic Problem-solving Questions

ISBN: 978-1-77149-202-7

Contents

Section 2:
Critical-thinking Questions

Level 1 – with hints

Level 2 – without hints

ISBN: 978-1-77149-202-7

ISBN: 978-1-77149-202-7

Section 1:
Basic Problem-solving Questions

ISBN: 978-1-77149-202-7

$$
\begin{array}{r}
\overset{1\ 1}{4358} \\
997 \\
\hline 5355
\end{array}
$$

③
$$
\begin{array}{r}
246 \\
+\ 3350 \\
\hline
\end{array}
$$

④
$$
\begin{array}{r}
\overset{1\ 1}{1298} \\
+\ 6408 \\
\hline 7706
\end{array}
$$

⑤
$$
\begin{array}{r}
4492 \\
+\ 1280 \\
\hline 5772
\end{array}
$$

⑥
$$
\begin{array}{r}
7211 \\
+\ 1271 \\
\hline 8482
\end{array}
$$

⑦
$$
\begin{array}{r}
8380 \\
+\ 579 \\
\hline 8959
\end{array}
$$

⑧
$$
\begin{array}{r}
\overset{1\ 1}{3649} \\
+\ 5287 \\
\hline 8936
\end{array}
$$

⑨ 768 + 2439 = _____

⑩ 3809 + 5624 = _____

⑪ 4588 + 1936 = _____

⑫ 8211 + 1069 = _____

⑬ 3407 + 4432 = _____

⑭ 6422 + 1646 = _____

⑮ 5286 + 1679 = _____

⑯ 7697 + 1516 = _____

⑰ 3495 + 3442 = _____

⑱ 7215 + 1230 = _____

⑲ 5740 + 2856 = _____

⑳ Find the totals.

a.

2106 mL
355 mL

_____ mL

b.

3468 g
1724 g

_____ g

c.
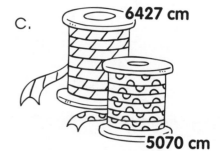
6427 cm
5070 cm

_____ cm

ISBN: 978-1-77149-202-7

Problem Solving

Try This!

A watermelon weighs 3459 g and a pineapple weighs 1799 g. What is the total weight?

Solution:

Step 1: Write a number sentence.

3459 + 1799 = [   ]

Step 2: Do the addition.

```
  3 4 5 9
+ 1 7 9 9
─────────
[        ]
```

Always include the unit in the concluding sentence.

Step 3: Write a concluding sentence.

The total weight is [   ] g.

① A factory produced 1733 green marbles and 3652 blue marbles. How many marbles did the factory produce in all?

The factory produced _____ marbles in all.

ISBN: 978-1-77149-202-7

② A charity received $3805 in donations in May and $2987 in June. How much money did the charity receive in total?

The charity received $ _____ in total.

③ Gary has bought a watermelon that weighs 2456 g and Gavin has bought one that is 1647 g heavier.

a. What is the weight of Gavin's watermelon?

The weight of Gavin's watermelon is _____ g.

b.

What is the total weight of our watermelons?

Gary

Gavin

The total weight is _____ g.

ISBN: 978-1-77149-202-7

④

I'm mixing 1912 mL of apple juice with 1048 mL of orange juice to make a jug of fruit punch.

Rachel

a. How much fruit punch will there be in the jug?

There will be _____ mL of fruit punch in the jug.

b. Rachel will make another jug of fruit punch with the same amount of juice. How much fruit punch will Rachel make in total?

Rachel will make _____ mL of fruit punch in total.

⑤ A factory produces 2750 cookies in an hour. How many cookies does it produce in 3 hours?

Tips

You can add 3 numbers in a vertical addition.

e.g.
$$\begin{array}{r} 15 \\ 15 \\ + 15 \\ \hline 45 \end{array}$$

The factory produces _____ cookies in 3 hours.

ISBN: 978-1-77149-202-7

⑥

4096 women attended a basketball game. There were 496 more men than women at the game.

How many people were at the game?

_____

⑦ Rosanna recorded the distances she biked last week in the chart. How far did she bike

a. on the weekend?

Distances Biked Last Week

Day	Distance (m)
Mon	1710
Tue	—
Wed	3417
Thu	—
Fri	3229
Sat	2870
Sun	2593

_____

b. on the weekdays?

_____

c. last week?

_____

ISBN: 978-1-77149-202-7

⑧ Three children played a video game. Their scores were recorded in the chart.

a. Find the total score of each child.

- Abby:

Children's Scores

Name / Round	Abby	Ben	Cory
1	3469	4203	3761
2	2964	3703	1694
3	5691	3780	6245

- Ben:
- Cory:

b.

In Round 4, Abby, Ben, and I had a score of 2419, 2507, and 2468 respectively.

Who had the highest total score and won the game?

ISBN: 978-1-77149-202-7

⑨ Canadarm2, the replacement for Canadarm, is 1231 kg heavier. What is the weight of Canadarm2?

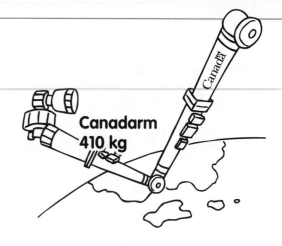

Canadarm
410 kg

_____

⑩ A hippo weighs 1805 kg and an elephant weighs 3621 kg more. What is the weight of the elephant?

_____

⑪ Martin mixes 4647 mL of red paint and 5209 mL of blue paint to make purple paint. How much purple paint does he have?

_____

⑫ The Byzantine Empire began around the year 330 and lasted for 1123 years. When did the Byzantine Empire end?

You may add or subtract years.
e.g.

2016 + 5 = 2021

_____

⑬ Ken consumes about 2631 mg of potassium per day. To meet the recommended daily amount, he needs to consume another 2069 mg of potassium. What is the recommended daily potassium intake?

_____

                                       ISBN: 978-1-77149-202-7

⑭ The speed of sound is 1225 km/h. An aircraft flying at supersonic speed is going 4798 km/h faster than the speed of sound. What is the speed of the aircraft?

_____

⑮ *The Odyssey* is a Greek epic poem of 11 210 lines. Its prequel, *The Iliad*, has 3583 more lines. How many lines does *The Iliad* have?

_____

⑯ Jasmine ran a 2462-m route. When she returned, she took a detour that was 968 m longer than the route. How far did she run in total?

_____

⑰ Mitchell consumed 2318 calories on Wednesday, and 2117 calories on both Thursday and Friday. How many calories did he consume in total?

_____

⑱ Calgary has an annual average precipitation of 419 mm; Vancouver has 1038 mm more than Calgary; St. John's has 77 mm more than Vancouver. What is the annual average precipitation in St. John's?

_____

ISBN: 978-1-77149-202-7

Subtraction

solving a variety of word problems that involve the subtraction of 4-digit numbers

 Math Skills

①
```
  6207
-  439
```

②
```
  3156
- 2218
```

③
```
  5498
- 1974
```

④
```
  3259
-  648
```

⑤
```
  4633
- 3847
```

⑥
```
  6448
- 2681
```

⑦
```
  4428
- 3492
```

⑧
```
  5982
- 4569
```

⑨ 5803 – 1975 = _____

⑩ 6253 – 5513 = _____

⑪ 9119 – 7041 = _____

⑫ 4359 – 1193 = _____

⑬ 2109 – 1738 = _____

⑭ 7428 – 2672 = _____

⑮ 7492 – 5309 = _____

⑯ 5706 – 3317 = _____

⑰ 8681 – 3412 = _____

⑱ 9688 – 6033 = _____

⑲ 6450 – 1669 = _____

⑳ Find the differences.

a.  **3016 mL** **Milk** **1009 mL** _____ mL

b.  **2810 cm** **926 cm** _____ cm

c. **1760 g** 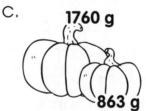 **863 g** _____ g

d. **2698 kg** **1187 kg** _____ kg

ISBN: 978-1-77149-202-7

Problem Solving

A farmer harvested 5432 apples last year and 4987 apples this year. What is the difference between the number of apples harvested?

Solution:

Step 1: Write a number sentence.

5432 – 4987 = ▭

> When finding the difference, subtract the smaller number from the bigger number.

Step 2: Do the subtraction.

```
   5432
 – 4987
 ──────
```

Step 3: Write a concluding sentence.

The difference is ▭ apples.

① There are 3669 apples in an apple orchard. How many apples will be left after 2408 apples are picked?

There will be _____ apples left.

ISBN: 978-1-77149-202-7

②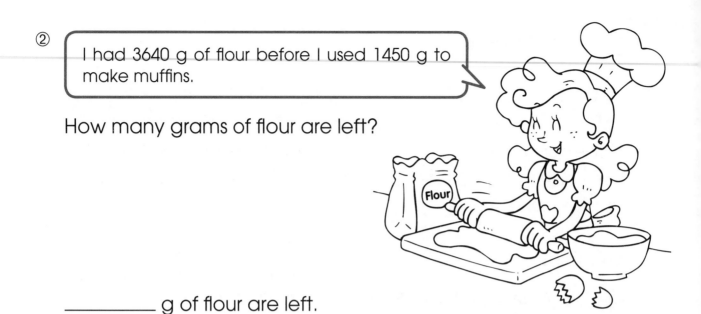

I had 3640 g of flour before I used 1450 g to make muffins.

How many grams of flour are left?

_____ g of flour are left.

③ A printing company needs to print 6000 brochures with its 8 printing machines. 3617 brochures are already printed. How many more brochures need to be printed?

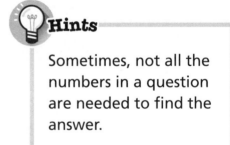

Hints

Sometimes, not all the numbers in a question are needed to find the answer.

_____ more brochures need to be printed.

④ Printing 5000 newsletters in colour costs $4749. If it costs $1548 less to print them in black and white, how much does it cost to print the newsletters in black and white?

It costs $ _____ to print the newsletters in black and white.

ISBN: 978-1-77149-202-7

⑤ Marcus poured 4524 mL of water into a bucket. After he left the bucket in the sun, only 3944 mL of water remained. How much water evaporated?

_____ mL of water evaporated.

⑥ At an arcade, Louisa got a score of 7551 points, beating her previous score of 6949 points.

a. By how many points did Louisa beat her previous score?

Louisa beat her previous score by _____ points.

b.

> I need a score of 8600 points to win this game.

How many more points does Louisa need to win?

Louisa

ARCADE

Louisa needs _____ more points to win.

ISBN: 978-1-77149-202-7

⑦ The height of a plant has been recorded over 4 years.

a. How much had the plant grown from Year 1 to Year 2?

Heights of a Plant

Year	Height (mm)
1	1397
2	1759
3	2089
4	2801

_____

b. Between which years did the plant grow the most?

_____

⑧ Dwayne is training for a marathon.

a. Dwayne needs to run 10 000 m. He has run 3075 m so far. How many more metres does he need to run?

_____

b.

I ran 4583 m in the first 30 minutes and 3684 m in the next 30 minutes.

How many more metres did Dwayne run in the first 30 minutes?

Dwayne

_____

ISBN: 978-1-77149-202-7

⑨ Bernice skied down from the top of a mountain that has an elevation of 3706 m.

> I skied down in 2 trips of 866 m and 789 m. What is my current elevation?

Bernice

_____

⑩ The regular price of a fridge is $5495 and a stove is $4162.

   a. The fridge goes on sale and is $2178 cheaper. How much is the fridge now?

_____

   b. The sale price of the stove is now $3086. How much cheaper is the stove than before?

_____

   c. What is the difference between the sale prices of the fridge and the stove?

_____

ISBN: 978-1-77149-202-7

⑪ A regular-sized bag of chips has 1568 calories and a party-sized bag has 2672 calories. How many more calories does the party-sized bag have?

_____

⑫ The file size of a video was reduced to 3280 MB from 5769 MB by lowering the resolution. By how much was the file size reduced?

Tips

MB means megabyte. It is a measuring unit for the size of a digital file.

_____

⑬ The Trans-Canada Highway is 7821 km long. Kelly drove 2714 km along it. What is the length of the Trans-Canada Highway that Kelly did not drive along?

_____

⑭ A household uses an annual average of 11 737 kWh of electricity in Canada and 6201 kWh in France. How much more electricity does a Canadian household use?

_____

⑮ In the United States, 10 511 solar panels were sold in 2009 and 7948 solar panels were sold in 2000. How many more solar panels were sold in 2009 than 2000?

_____

ISBN: 978-1-77149-202-7

⑯ The maximum weight of a piece of carry-on luggage is 10 000 g. Michelle's bag weighs 8253 g. How much weight can Michelle add to her bag at most?

_____

⑰ An airplane is cruising at an altitude of 12 184 m above sea level. To prepare for landing, it must go below 4600 m. By at least how much must the airplane decrease its altitude?

_____

⑱ One year, there were 6291 forest fires in Canada. 2670 of them can be attributed to human activities and 1614 to lightning. How many forest fires do not have a known cause?

_____

⑲ The average depth of the Pacific Ocean is 10 911 m, which is 2864 m deeper than the Indian Ocean. What is the average depth of the Atlantic Ocean if it is 4708 m shallower than the Indian Ocean?

_____

⑳ How much more is saved on the couch than on the table?

Furniture SALE

$3206 ~~$2889~~

$4289 ~~$3618~~

_____

Multiplication

solving a variety of word problems that involve the multiplication of 2- and 3-digit numbers

Math Skills

①
$$
\begin{array}{r}
33 \\
\times9 \\
\hline
\end{array}
$$

②
$$
\begin{array}{r}
67 \\
\times5 \\
\hline
\end{array}
$$

③
$$
\begin{array}{r}
108 \\
\times3 \\
\hline
\end{array}
$$

④
$$
\begin{array}{r}
225 \\
\times6 \\
\hline
\end{array}
$$

⑤
$$
\begin{array}{r}
56 \\
\times12 \\
\hline
\end{array}
$$

⑥
$$
\begin{array}{r}
13 \\
\times49 \\
\hline
\end{array}
$$

⑦
$$
\begin{array}{r}
31 \\
\times86 \\
\hline
\end{array}
$$

⑧
$$
\begin{array}{r}
52 \\
\times63 \\
\hline
\end{array}
$$

⑨ 67×8 = _____

⑩ 73×2 = _____

⑪ 83×6 = _____

⑫ 169×8 = _____

⑬ 242×5 = _____

⑭ 671×7 = _____

⑮ 46×22 = _____

⑯ 81×13 = _____

⑰ 51×60 = _____

⑱ 33×28 = _____

⑲ 17×43 = _____

⑳ 62×98 = _____

㉑

a. 25 cartons: _____ × _____ = _____ (eggs)

b. 100 cartons: _____ × _____ = _____ (eggs)

㉒

a. 36 boxes: _____ × _____ = _____ (pencils)

b. 60 boxes: _____ × _____ = _____ (pencils)

ISBN: 978-1-77149-202-7

 **Problem Solving**

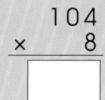

Alex baked 104 cookies. If each cookie has 8 chocolate chips, how many chocolate chips did Alex use?

Solution:

Step 1: Write a number sentence.

$104 \times 8 =$ [ ]

Step 2: Do the multiplication.

$$
\begin{array}{r}
104 \\
\times \quad 8 \\
\hline

\end{array}
$$

> Remember to align the ones digits.

Step 3: Write a concluding sentence.

Alex used [ ] chocolate chips.

① 128 cranberries are needed to make a bottle of cranberry juice. How many cranberries are needed to make 6 bottles of cranberry juice?

_____ cranberries are needed.

ISBN: 978-1-77149-202-7

② A juice box has 200 mL of juice. How much juice is there in a package of 8 juice boxes?

There is _____ mL of juice.

③ A bag of trail mix weighs 596 g. What is the weight of 3 bags of trail mix?

The weight of 3 bags of trail mix is _____ g.

④ A vending machine sells bags of chips for $2 each. How much money will the vending machine receive if it sells 216 bags of chips?

By the commutative property, 2 x 216 is the same as 216 x 2.

The vending machine will receive $ _____ .

ISBN: 978-1-77149-202-7

⑤ One bouquet has a dozen roses. How many roses are there in a dozen bouquets?

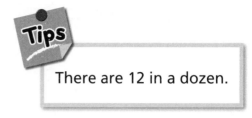

Tips

There are 12 in a dozen.

There are _____ roses.

⑥ There are 34 rows of 26 seats in a theatre. Each theatre ticket costs $8.

a. How many seats are there in the theatre?

There are _____ seats in the theatre.

b.
How much will it cost to buy all the theatre tickets?

It will cost $ _____ .

⑦ A robot-building club has 11 members. Each member builds 27 robots for a fundraising event.

a. How many robots are built?

_____

b. 100 mL of paint is needed for each robot.

How much paint is needed in total?

_____

⑧ Michael eats 45 raisins every day. How many raisins will he eat in January?

Tips

There are 31 days in January.

_____

⑨ A book series has 4101 pages. If Olivia reads 10 pages a day, will she finish the series in a year with 365 days?

_____

ISBN: 978-1-77149-202-7

⑩ Jasper is deciding between buying 3 different packages of chocolates.

- Package 1: 4 boxes of 10 chocolate eggs
- Package 2: 2 boxes of 4 chocolate bunnies
- Package 3: 10 boxes of 3 chocolate bars

The packages all cost the same. Which package of chocolates should Jasper buy to get the most chocolate?

⑪ Lawrence folds 15 paper stars each day.

a. How many paper stars does he fold in 2 weeks?

b. Each paper star is made from a 9-cm strip of paper. Is a roll of 18-m paper enough to make 2 weeks' worth of stars?

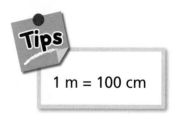

1 m = 100 cm

ISBN: 978-1-77149-202-7

⑫ 16 students from each school are selected for a swim meet. There are 53 schools participating in the swim meet.

a. How many students are at the swim meet?

_____

b. The students are scheduled to swim in 70 races with 12 students in each race. Are all the students scheduled to race?

_____

c. For the students who are participating, an entrance fee of $5 is required per student. How much money is collected in total?

_____

⑬ An elevator has a maximum weight limit of 1164 kg.

a. If an average person weighs 76 kg, can 16 people ride the elevator?

_____

b. How much weight can the elevator carry in 5 trips?

_____

ISBN: 978-1-77149-202-7

⑭ A city transit system operates 64 buses. Each bus can carry a maximum of 66 passengers.

    a. What is the maximum number of passengers if all the buses run at the same time?

    _____

    b. If the city replaces the buses with 40 streetcars that can each carry 108 passengers, will the maximum number of passengers increase or decrease?

    _____

⑮ A truck can travel up to 76 km in an hour. Can it travel 1000 km in 13 hours?

_____

⑯ Royal Concert Hall has 28 rows of 56 seats and Alexander Music Hall has 34 rows of 45 seats. Which venue has a higher capacity?

_____

⑰

3 participants are each awarded a $75 prize every night. How much money will be awarded after 6 nights?

_____

Division

solving a variety of word problems that involve the division of 3- and 4-digit numbers by 1-digit numbers

 Math Skills

①
$$6 \overline{)300}$$

②
$$9 \overline{)819}$$

③
$$4 \overline{)268}$$

④
$$5 \overline{)457}$$

⑤
$$6 \overline{)796}$$

⑥
$$3 \overline{)687}$$

⑦
$$2 \overline{)2408}$$

⑧
$$4 \overline{)4148}$$

⑨ $295 \div 3$ = _____

⑩ $489 \div 6$ = _____

⑪ $372 \div 4$ = _____

⑫ $960 \div 5$ = _____

⑬ $187 \div 6$ = _____

⑭ $863 \div 8$ = _____

⑮ $201 \div 9$ = _____

⑯ $714 \div 8$ = _____

⑰ $1996 \div 8$ = _____

⑱ $2018 \div 7$ = _____

⑲ $1049 \div 7$ = _____

⑳ $5025 \div 5$ = _____

㉑ $2207 \div 6$ = _____

㉒ Find the number of oranges in each carton if they are divided into

a. 7 cartons: _____ = _____ (oranges)

b. 8 cartons: _____ = _____

504 oranges

ISBN: 978-1-77149-202-7

Problem Solving

Try This!

Each shirt needs 8 buttons. If a tailor has 112 buttons, how many shirts can be made?

Solution:

Step 1: Write a number sentence.

$$112 \div 8 = \boxed{}$$

Step 2: Do the division.

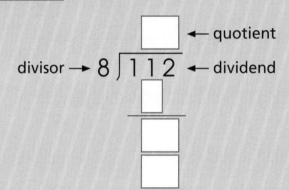

$$\boxed{} \leftarrow \text{quotient}$$

divisor $\rightarrow 8 \overline{)112} \leftarrow$ dividend

In division, a dividend is divided by a divisor. The answer that results is called a quotient. Sometimes, an answer has a remainder too.

Step 3: Write a concluding sentence.

$\boxed{}$ shirts can be made.

① Thea has 133 books in 7 equal stacks. How many books are there in each stack?

There are _____ books in each stack.

ISBN: 978-1-77149-202-7

② Rebecca has 231 crayons. She wants to share them evenly among herself and 6 of her friends. How many crayons will each person get?

Hints

Don't forget to include Rebecca when counting the number of people to divide by.

Each person will get _____ crayons.

③ A machine sorts 8000 jelly beans equally into 10 jars.

a. How many jelly beans are there in each jar?

There are _____ jelly beans in each jar.

b.

I put the jelly beans from one of the jars into 100 packages.

How many jelly beans are there in each package?

There are _____ jelly beans in each package.

ISBN: 978-1-77149-202-7

④
> I have 175 cherries. Each serving of cherry pie requires 6 cherries.

How many servings can Chef Francis make?

Chef Francis

Chef Francis can make _____ servings.

⑤ Sandra wants to put 237 pickled eggs into jars. If each jar holds 5 eggs, how many jars does Sandra need to hold all of the eggs?

Hints

Any remaining pickled eggs will need another jar.

Sandra needs _____ jars.

⑥ Josephine skates 7640 cm in 8 seconds. How far does she skate each second on average?

Josephine skates _____ cm each second on average.

ISBN: 978-1-77149-202-7

⑦

I need to wrap 9 gifts with equal lengths of ribbons.

If Layla has 4515 cm of ribbon, how much ribbon can be used for each gift?

Layla

_____

⑧ Three friends found a missing cat and they were rewarded $500. They split the reward evenly and gave the remainder to charity. How much did each person get and how much went to charity?

_____

⑨ Angela's bakery made $1470 from the sales of cookies in one week. Each cookie cost $5 and the cookies were sold in bags of 6.

a. On average, how much money was made in one day?

_____

b. On average, how many bags of cookies were sold each day?

_____

ISBN: 978-1-77149-202-7

⑩ Thomas's toy blocks weigh 1743 g.

a. If each toy block weighs 3 g, how many toy blocks are there?

_____

b.

| I can combine 8 toy blocks to make 1 big block. |

How many big blocks can Thomas make?

Thomas

_____

⑪ Dan and 4 friends split a $163 dinner bill. They each paid more for the tip. If they did not have coins in cents, at least how much did each person pay?

_____

⑫ 5426 cobs of corn are split among 4 trucks for transport. The corn is split as evenly as possible. How many cobs of corn does each truck have?

Hints

To split evenly, any remainders should be spread among the trucks.

⑬ There are 627 beets and they are to be divided into packs of 4.

a. How many more beets are needed so that there are no leftovers?

_____

b. If the beets are divided into packs of 8 instead, how many more beets are needed so that there are no leftovers?

_____

⑭ The students have collected $3640 to buy pizza for their school. Each slice of pizza costs $6 and there are 8 slices in one pizza.

a. How many slices of pizza can the students afford?

_____

b. If only whole pizzas can be ordered, how many pizzas can the students order?

_____

⑮ A coffee machine holds 8400 mL of coffee and dispenses 100 mL for each cup. Its coffee filter is rinsed after every 7 cups. How many times does the filter need to be rinsed before the machine is refilled?

_____

ISBN: 978-1-77149-202-7

⑯ Gary splits 1771 beans into 8 jars and Ashley splits 809 beans into 4 jars.

a. Who has more beans in each jar? Who has more leftover beans?

_____

b. They each further divide one of their jars into 5, 6, or 7 piles. If they both have the same number of beans left, how many piles do they each split their beans into?

_____

⑰ Jason wants to display his 1000 marbles evenly in a number of vases. He can use up to 9 vases.

a. If he has 4 leftover marbles, how many vases does he use?

_____

b. How many vases can Jason use so that there are no leftover marbles?

_____

⑱ 2000 potatoes are to be sorted into bags of 6, 7, or 8 potatoes. Which number of potatoes in a bag will have no leftovers?

_____

ISBN: 978-1-77149-202-7

Fractions

solving a variety of word problems that involve converting and comparing fractions

 Math Skills

① Write two equivalent fractions for each.

a. 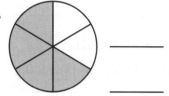 ___ ___

b. 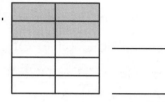 ___

c. 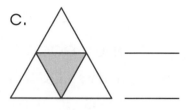 ___

d. 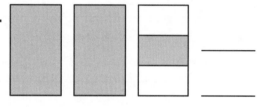 ___ ___

e. 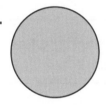 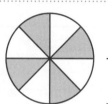 ___

② Circle the greater fractions.

a. $\dfrac{2}{4}$ $\dfrac{3}{4}$ b. $\dfrac{4}{5}$ $\dfrac{2}{5}$ c. $\dfrac{7}{8}$ $\dfrac{3}{4}$ d. $\dfrac{2}{5}$ $\dfrac{6}{10}$

e. $\dfrac{4}{6}$ $\dfrac{4}{7}$ f. $\dfrac{5}{8}$ $\dfrac{5}{10}$ g. $1\dfrac{1}{2}$ $\dfrac{3}{4}$ h. $\dfrac{6}{5}$ $\dfrac{3}{5}$

i. $1\dfrac{6}{10}$ $2\dfrac{3}{5}$ j. $\dfrac{16}{5}$ $3\dfrac{1}{3}$ k. $\dfrac{17}{3}$ $\dfrac{21}{5}$ l. $\dfrac{20}{7}$ $2\dfrac{1}{3}$

③ Put the fractions in order from least to greatest.

a. $\dfrac{4}{7}$ $\dfrac{5}{7}$ $\dfrac{3}{7}$ $\dfrac{1}{7}$ b. $\dfrac{6}{9}$ $\dfrac{1}{3}$ $\dfrac{5}{9}$ $\dfrac{4}{3}$

_____   _____

c. $\dfrac{7}{8}$ $\dfrac{3}{4}$ $1\dfrac{1}{2}$ $\dfrac{5}{4}$ d. $\dfrac{14}{4}$ $1\dfrac{1}{2}$ $\dfrac{9}{2}$ $\dfrac{17}{4}$

_____   _____

ISBN: 978-1-77149-202-7

Problem Solving

Alan ate $\frac{1}{8}$ of a pancake and Steve ate $\frac{2}{8}$ of it. Who ate more of the pancake?

Solution:

Step 1: **Draw a diagram for each fraction.**

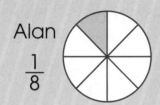

Alan $\frac{1}{8}$ Steve $\frac{2}{8}$

Fractions can also be represented using rectangles. They are easier to divide into equal parts than circles.

Step 2: **Compare the fractions.**

$\frac{1}{8}$ ☐ $\frac{2}{8}$

Step 3: **Write a concluding sentence.**

☐ ate more of the pancake.

① Kayleen ate $\frac{1}{6}$ of a pie and Keith ate $\frac{2}{6}$ of it. Who ate $\frac{1}{3}$ of the pie?

_____ ate $\frac{1}{3}$ of the pie.

ISBN: 978-1-77149-202-7

②

I have finished $\frac{3}{4}$ of my homework and Eric has finished $\frac{1}{2}$ of his.

Dave

Who has finished more of his homework?

_____ has finished more of his homework.

③ Miranda ran $\frac{3}{5}$ of the track and Wilson ran $\frac{7}{8}$ of the track.

a. Who ran more of the track?

Tips

You can compare the fractions on number lines to see which fraction is greater.

_____ ran more of the track.

b. Miranda's sister, Rachel, ran $\frac{6}{10}$ of the track. Whom did Rachel run less than?

Rachel ran less than _____ .

ISBN: 978-1-77149-202-7

④ A pizza was divided into 8 equal slices. Andrew ate 2 slices and his sister ate 1 slice. What fraction of the pizza is left?

_____ of the pizza is left.

⑤ Mr. Mendel did a survey on his class's favourite colour. $\frac{1}{3}$ of his class voted red, $\frac{1}{6}$ voted blue, and $\frac{1}{2}$ voted yellow. Which colour had the most votes? Which colour had the fewest votes?

Hints

Divide a diagram into 6 equal parts to find the answers.

_____ had the most votes and _____ had the fewest

votes.

⑥ Jessica is making a jug of fruit punch.

$\frac{1}{4}$ of it is lime juice, $\frac{5}{8}$ of it is orange juice, and $\frac{1}{8}$ of it is soda.

Which ingredient does the fruit punch have the most of?

The ingredient is _____ .

ISBN: 978-1-77149-202-7

43

⑦ A pepperoni pizza was cut into 10 equal slices. A vegetarian pizza of the same size was cut into 6 equal slices.

I ate 2 slices of each pizza.

Cynthia

a. Which pizza did Cynthia eat more of?

_____

b. A Hawaiian pizza was cut into 8 equal slices. If Cynthia ate more of it than the pepperoni pizza but less than the vegetarian pizza, what fraction of the Hawaiian pizza did Cynthia eat?

_____

⑧ The Marco Pizzeria divides all their pizzas into 6 equal slices.

a. If 15 slices were sold today, how many pizzas were sold?

Hints

Convert improper fractions into mixed numbers first.

_____

b. Yesterday, $2\frac{4}{6}$ pizzas were sold. On which day were more pizzas sold?

_____

ISBN: 978-1-77149-202-7

⑨ Daniel has read $1\frac{1}{2}$ books and his brother has read $\frac{7}{6}$ books. Who has read more?

_____

⑩ Lisa ran $\frac{11}{5}$ laps around the school today and $\frac{11}{3}$ laps yesterday.

Did she run more laps today or yesterday?

Hints

When comparing fractions that have the same numerator, the fraction with the smaller denominator is greater.

_____

⑪ Teresa surveyed her friends about their favourite day of the week.

Day of the Week	Mon	Tue	Wed	Thu	Fri	Sat	Sun
Number of Votes	0	1	3	2	5	8	6

a. What fraction of her friends voted for Tuesday?

_____

b. What fraction of her friends voted for a weekend?

_____

c. Which day has $\frac{8}{25}$ of the votes?

_____

d. Which day has $\frac{1}{5}$ of the votes?

_____

⑫

I have 10 balloons; 6 of them are red, 2 are blue, and the rest are green.

a. What fraction of the balloons are green?

_____

b. What fraction of the balloons are not green?

_____

⑬ Lydia gave away 6 of her 20 cookies. What fraction of her cookies does she still have?

_____

⑭ Ben is on a game show and he has to choose between getting $\frac{5}{6}$ or $\frac{7}{8}$ of a prize.

a. Which is the better choice?

_____

b. Later, Ben is given an option of getting $\frac{9}{10}$ of a prize. Should he give up his previous choice?

_____

ISBN: 978-1-77149-202-7

⑮ Three friends are having a race and their times are as follows:

Bonnie: $\frac{13}{4}$ minutes   Connie: $\frac{16}{6}$ minutes   Donnie: $\frac{27}{8}$ minutes

In what order did the friends cross the finish line?

_____

⑯ Evan and Sarah are on a scavenger hunt. Evan found $\frac{77}{100}$ of the clues and Sarah found $\frac{33}{50}$ of the clues.

a. Who is closer to finishing the scavenger hunt?

_____

b. A while later, out of 100 clues, Sarah found 12 more clues. Who is closer to finishing the scavenger hunt now?

_____

⑰ A robot weighs $2\frac{7}{10}$ g more than a teddy bear, and a doll weighs $\frac{22}{7}$ g more than the teddy bear.

a. Which weighs more, the robot or the doll?

_____

b. A toy truck weighs $\frac{11}{3}$ g less than the robot. Order the toys from lightest to heaviest.

_____

ISBN: 978-1-77149-202-7

Decimals

solving a variety of word problems that involve addition and subtraction of decimals to 1 decimal place

 Math Skills

①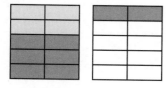

0.4 + 0.8 = _____

②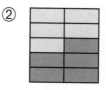

0.5 + 0.6 = _____

③

1.6 – 0.6 = _____

④

1.8 – 0.9 = _____

⑤

1.7 – 1.3 = _____

⑥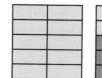

1.4 + 0.5 = _____

⑦
$$\begin{array}{r} 4.2 \\ +\ 3.7 \\ \hline \end{array}$$

⑧
$$\begin{array}{r} 8.4 \\ +\ 6.1 \\ \hline \end{array}$$

⑨
$$\begin{array}{r} 5.1 \\ +\ 7.2 \\ \hline \end{array}$$

⑩
$$\begin{array}{r} 7.2 \\ -\ 3.8 \\ \hline \end{array}$$

⑪
$$\begin{array}{r} 8.7 \\ -\ 5.9 \\ \hline \end{array}$$

⑫
$$\begin{array}{r} 11.3 \\ -\ 7.7 \\ \hline \end{array}$$

⑬
$$\begin{array}{r} 6.4 \\ +\ 4.6 \\ \hline \end{array}$$

⑭
$$\begin{array}{r} 10.0 \\ -\ 1.5 \\ \hline \end{array}$$

⑮ 7.3 + 4.7 = _____

⑯ 8.7 – 4.2 = _____

⑰ 5.4 + 3.8 = _____

⑱ 11.3 + 2.6 = _____

⑲ 8.7 – 4.2 = _____

⑳ 6.9 – 3.7 = _____

㉑ 14.3 – 4.8 = _____

㉒ 12.7 + 13.2 = _____

㉓ 17.9 – 14.8 = _____

㉔ 20 – 4.5 = _____

ISBN: 978-1-77149-202-7

Problem Solving

 **Try This!**

Janice used 1.4 m of ribbon to tie a gift and 0.8 m of ribbon to tie its bow. How much ribbon did Janice use?

Solution:

Step 1: **Write a number sentence.**

1.4 + 0.8 = ☐

Make sure the decimal points are aligned when adding or subtracting decimals.

Step 2: **Do the addition.**

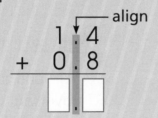

Step 3: **Write a concluding sentence.**

Janice used ☐ m of ribbon in total.

① Danny mixes 0.6 kg of cocoa powder and 0.8 kg of sugar to make chocolate milk powder. How much chocolate milk powder does Danny make?

Danny makes _____ kg of chocolate milk powder.

ISBN: 978-1-77149-202-7

② Sam's bowling ball is 4.1 kg. Selina's bowling ball is 0.9 kg lighter. What is the weight of Selina's bowling ball?

Selina's bowling ball is _____ kg.

③ It takes 6.2 hours to get from Toronto to Montreal by car.

a. How long does a round trip take by car?

Hints

A "round trip" means travelling to a place and back.

A round trip takes _____ hours by car.

b.

Travelling by train takes 4.9 hours each way. How much faster is travelling by train than by car?

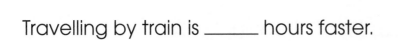

Travelling by train is _____ hours faster.

ISBN: 978-1-77149-202-7

④ Jack swam 3 laps and recorded his time for each lap. How long did it take Jack to swim 3 laps?

Jack's Swimming Record

Lap	Time (minutes)
1	2.1
2	1.6
3	1.9

It took Jack _____ minutes to swim 3 laps.

⑤ A trail is divided into 3 sections. The first section is 7.8 km long and the second section is 2.7 km longer.

a. How long is the second section?

The second section is _____ km long.

b. 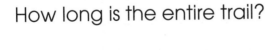 The third section is 1.9 km shorter than the first section.

How long is the entire trail?

Hints

Find the length of the third section first.

The entire trail is _____ km long.

⑥

> I'm climbing a 16.7-m wall and I need to climb 3.4 m more to reach the top.

Chris

a. How much has Chris climbed?

_____

b. Chris climbs down the wall after he reaches the top. How much more does he need to climb down if he has already climbed down 6.9 m?

_____

⑦ Mr. Leung has two aquariums that have capacities of 20.8 L and 56.8 L.

a. What is the total capacity of Mr. Leung's aquariums?

_____

b. Mr. Leung replaces his two aquariums with one big aquarium that has a capacity of 94.6 L. How much more water can he add to the new aquarium?

_____

ISBN: 978-1-77149-202-7

⑧ In a shot put competition, Randy's throw was 17.3 m, which was 2.7 m farther than last year.

a. How far did Randy throw last year?

_____

b.

My current record is 5.8 m less than the world record.

What is the world record for shot put?

_____

⑨ Shawn ran 3 laps around the school which took him 43.2 seconds, 45.7 seconds, and 51.9 seconds to complete.

a. What was Shawn's total time?

_____

b. Beverly's total time was the same as Shawn's. It took her 38.5 seconds and 44.6 seconds to run the first two laps. What was Beverly's time for the third lap?

_____

ISBN: 978-1-77149-202-7

⑩ Robert fills 3 soap dispensers with a capacity of 0.7 L each with the family-sized bag of hand soap.

a. How much hand soap is left in the bag?

_____

b. Robert mixes the remaining soap with some water to dilute it to make 3.1 L of soap. How much water is used?

_____

⑪ In a skiing competition, Mary completed the race in 21.6 min and Louise was 1.9 min slower than Mary. What was Nelson's time if he beat Louise's time by 2.4 min?

_____

⑫ There are two paths from Anne's house to her school.

a. Which path is shorter? How long is it?

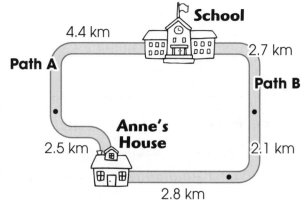

_____

b. A shortcut from Anne's house to her school is 3.7 km shorter than the longer path. How long is the shortcut?

_____

ISBN: 978-1-77149-202-7

⑬ The Leaning Tower of Pisa has 2 heights because of its tilt. What is the difference between the 2 heights?

56.7 m

55.9 m

_____

⑭ A truck weighs 9.4 tonnes and can carry 18.2 tonnes including its own weight.

a. How many tonnes of cargo can a truck carry in 2 trips?

_____

b. Can 4 trucks carry 70 tonnes in 2 trips?

_____

⑮ At a gymnastics competition, Natalie earned the scores of 7.6, 6.3, 7.2, 7.4, and 6.8. The highest and the lowest scores were dropped and the rest were added together to get the final score.

a. What was Natalie's final score?

_____

b. If Natalie got a penalty that lowered her 7.6 score by 0.3, what would have been her final score?

Hints

The scores that were dropped have changed.

_____

ISBN: 978-1-77149-202-7

7 Money

solving a variety of word problems that involve adding and subtracting money amounts

Math Skills

① **A**

$ [   ]

B

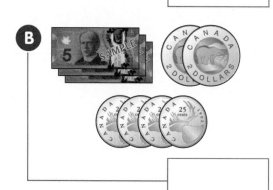

[   ]

C

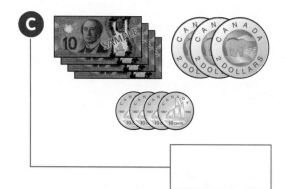

[   ]

D

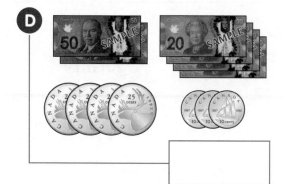

[   ]

② Find the totals.

a. **A** and **B**

_____ + _____ = _____

b. **B** and **C**

_____

c. **B** and **D**

_____

d. **C** and **D**

_____

③ Find the differences.

a. **A** and **C**

_____ – _____ = _____

b. **B** and **C**

_____

c. **B** and **D**

_____

d. **C** and **D**

_____

56

ISBN: 978-1-77149-202-7

Problem Solving

Mrs. Hudson bought a scarf for $24.50 and a hat for $45.20. How much did Mrs. Hudson pay altogether?

Solution:

Step 1: **Write a number sentence.**

$24.50 + $45.20 = ☐

The decimal point in the answer must align with the decimals that are being added or subtracted.

Step 2: **Do the addition.**

```
  24.50
+ 45.20
───────
```

Step 3: **Write a concluding sentence.**

Mrs. Hudson paid $ ☐ altogether.

① Jean earned $36.20 last week and $40.50 this week. How much more did Jean earn this week?

Jean earned $ _____ more this week.

ISBN: 978-1-77149-202-7

② How much more money does Leonard need to buy a toy car that costs $50?

Leonard's Savings

Leonard needs $ _____ more.

③ Freddie has 5 $10 bills, 6 loonies, 1 quarter, and 3 nickels. He needs $7.30 more to buy a video game.

a. How much does the video game cost?

Whenever a number of bills and/or coins are given, find their total value first.

The video game costs $ _____ .

b.

Doug has lent me 2 $5 bills to buy the video game. How much money will I have left after buying the game?

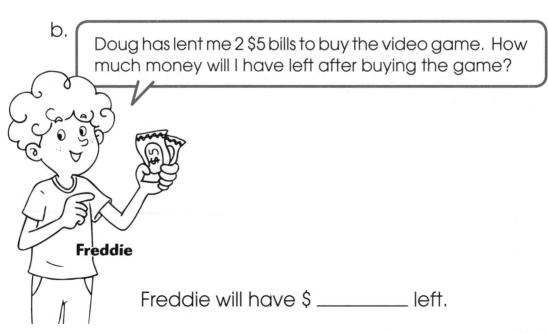

Freddie

Freddie will have $ _____ left.

ISBN: 978-1-77149-202-7

④ At a theatre, a movie ticket costs $11.25 and a bag of popcorn costs $8.60.

    a. How much did it cost Kyle to buy 2 tickets and a bag of popcorn?

      It cost Kyle $ _____ .

    b. Kyle paid $35 and got 3 loonies, 2 quarters, and 4 nickels back. Did Kyle get back the correct change?

      Kyle _____ get back the correct change.
            _{did/did not}

⑤ If Isabella buys all three toys with a $50 bill, what are the fewest bills and coins she can get back in change?

$15.95

$6.40

$12.15

Isabella can get back _____

_____

ISBN: 978-1-77149-202-7

⑥ Jeffrey has $36.25 and Craig has $27.90. Jeffrey owes Craig $8.45.

   a. How much does each person have after Jeffrey pays back Craig?

_____

b.

> How much more money do I have than Jeffrey now?

_____

⑦ Judy paid $47.75 for a sweater and a shirt.

   a. How much did the sweater cost if the shirt cost $19.90?

_____

b. How much more would Judy have paid if she bought 2 sweaters instead?

_____

ISBN: 978-1-77149-202-7

⑧ Audrey and Millie have a total of $48.95.

Hints

Find Audrey's money amount before Millie gave her $1.35.

a. Millie had $24.70 and gave $1.35 to Audrey. How much does Audrey have now?

_____

b. Santos and the two girls have a total of $74.45. Does Santos have more money than Audrey?

_____

⑨ A $34.75 DVD is on sale for $21.60 and a $45.20 video game is on sale for $32.65.

a. Which item has a bigger price reduction?

_____

b. If Bobby buys both the DVD and the video game, how much will he save in total?

_____

ISBN: 978-1-77149-202-7

⑩ A regular movie ticket is $3.15 cheaper than a 3-D movie ticket. How much will 2 regular movie tickets cost if a 3-D movie ticket is $16.45?

_____

⑪ A road trip cost $78.20. $34.75 of it was spent on snacks and the rest was spent on gas. How much more was spent on gas than snacks?

_____

⑫ Jenny had 5 $20 bills and she spent $37.15 on a new backpack. She wants to buy a dress for $45.10 and a scarf for $33.20. How much more money does she need?

_____

⑬

I have $36.75. Penelope has 2 $20 bills, 4 toonies, 3 quarters, and 1 nickel.

Ella

a. How much money do Ella and Penelope have together?

_____

b. Do they have enough money to buy 3 cakes that cost $28.50 each?

_____

ISBN: 978-1-77149-202-7

⑭ Elizabeth earns $11.80 an hour and Jonathan earns $12.15 an hour. What is the difference between their earnings if Elizabeth works for 3 hours and Jonathan works for 2 hours?

_____

⑮ Ms. Johnson has $55 and wants to buy as many $15.35 notebooks as possible. How many notebooks can Ms. Johnson buy and how much will she have left?

_____

⑯ Mr. McNeil bought 3 books that cost him $18.75, $14.05, and $22.30. He got back $4.90 in change. How did he pay for the books if he only used 4 bills?

_____

⑰ A $45.95 pair of skates is on sale with $15.50 off. Renting a pair of skates costs $4.50 each time. If Bernard plans to skate 4 times, should he buy or rent skates?

_____

⑱ Paula had $100. She spent $56.25 of it on gas and $29.15 on groceries.

How many muffins can I buy with the remaining money?

$4.55 each

Paula

_____

ISBN: 978-1-77149-202-7

Time

solving a variety of word problems that involve converting between units of time and finding elapsed time

Math Skills

① 2 minutes = _____ seconds

② 240 seconds = _____ minutes

③ 4 hours = _____ minutes

④ 600 minutes = _____ hours

⑤ 3 weeks = _____ days

⑥ 2 weeks 4 days = _____ days

⑦ 72 hours = _____ days

⑧ 9 hours = _____ minutes

⑨ 3 years = _____ weeks

⑩ 5 centuries = _____ decades

⑪ 10 years = _____ months

⑫ 3 millenniums = _____ centuries

⑬ Write the times and find the elapsed times.

a.

Elapsed Time _____ h _____ min

b.

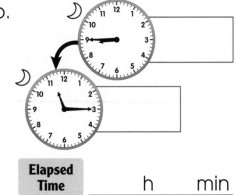

Elapsed Time _____ h _____ min

c. 6:45 p.m. → 8:28 p.m.

_____ h _____ min

d. 9:20 a.m. → 1:45 p.m.

_____ h _____ min

e. May 15, 2017 → May 27, 2017

_____ days

f. June 19, 2016 → July 9, 2017

_____ weeks

g. March 2011 → March 2015

_____ years

h. April 1, 2019 → July 1, 2019

_____ months

ISBN: 978-1-77149-202-7

Problem Solving

Vanessa wakes up at 7:15 a.m. and leaves for school at 8:05 a.m. How long does it take her to get ready for school?

Solution:

Step 1: Determine the start time and the end time.

Start time: 7:15 a.m.
End time: 8:05 a.m.

Remember these rules when adding or subtracting times.

Step 2: Do the subtraction.

$$\begin{array}{r} {}^{7}\!\!\not{8}:\not{0}5^{\,65} \\ -\ 7:15 \\ \hline \boxed{\quad:\quad} \end{array}$$

← Trade 1 h for 60 min.

- Add or subtract hours and minutes separately.
- Trade 1 hour for every 60 minutes.

Step 3: Write a concluding sentence.

It takes Vanessa ☐ minutes to get ready for school.

① Troy finished eating dinner at 7:05 p.m. His dinner lasted 45 minutes. What time did Troy start eating dinner?

Troy started eating dinner at _____ .

② A basketball game started at 6:40 p.m. and finished at 8:15 p.m.

a. How long was the basketball game?

The basketball game was _____ long.

b. The next basketball game is scheduled to start at 11:35 a.m. tomorrow. If the basketball game lasts for 2 hours and 15 minutes, what time will the game finish?

Tips

Remember that a.m. refers to the morning and p.m. refers to the evening.

The game will finish at _____ .

③

I started running at 9:32 a.m. and I crossed the finish line at 2:16 p.m.

How long did it take Marco to run the marathon?

Marco

It took Marco _____ to run the marathon.

 ISBN: 978-1-77149-202-7

④
I have signed up for a photography course. The course consists of 8 lessons of 45 minutes each.

What is the total duration of the course in hours?

The total duration of the course is _____ .

⑤ A train is scheduled to arrive at the station three and a half hours before noon.

a. What time does the train arrive?

Hints

"Noon" is 12:00 p.m.

The train arrives at _____ .

b. The last train leaves the station one hour and fifteen minutes after midnight. What time does the last train leave?

Hints

"Midnight" is 00:00 in 24-hour clock time.

The last train leaves at _____ .

ISBN: 978-1-77149-202-7

⑥ Ana is attending a concert at 7:55 p.m. It will take her 2 hours and 20 minutes to travel to the concert.

a. If Ana leaves at 5:30 p.m., will she arrive before the concert starts?

_____

b. What time should Ana leave if she wants to arrive 15 minutes before the concert starts?

_____

⑦ A 55-minute yoga class started at 7:30 a.m. Kendra was late and arrived 45 minutes before the class ended. What time did Kendra arrive?

_____

⑧

I am going on a cruise from May 28 to June 10.

For how many days will Patsy be on the cruise?

_____

ISBN: 978-1-77149-202-7

⑨

> The library is open from 8:00 a.m. to 7:30 p.m. on weekdays.
> It is open 2 and a half hours less on weekends.

a. For how many hours a day is the library
open on weekends?

_____

b. For how many hours is the library open
in 1 week?

_____

⑩ Denise signed up for a weekly exercise program on Wednesdays;
she started on March 9 and completed it on May 4.

a. How many classes were there?

_____

b. Denise wants to join the program again. If the program ends
on December 14, in which month does it begin?

_____

⑪ A leap year occurs once every 4 years. It has an extra day in February. At most, how many days are there in a decade?

Tips

A decade is 10 years.

_____

⑫ Roberta had 30 months left on the lease of her vehicle. When would her lease end if it was May 1, 2016?

_____

⑬ Mr. Turner gave his class a quiz 3 weeks and 2 days ago. When was the quiz if today is November 10?

_____

⑭ A computer anti-virus program is scheduled to perform a scan on the 7th of every month.

a. If today is August 14, how many days are there until the next scan?

Hints

Do not include the days of the scan when counting the number of days.

_____

b. How many scans will there be from August 14 to the end of the year?

_____

ISBN: 978-1-77149-202-7

⑮ Vernon is travelling by plane from Montreal to New York with a stopover in Toronto.

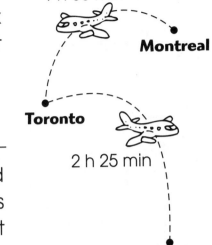

1 h 35 min

Montreal

Toronto

2 h 25 min

New York

   a. When does Vernon arrive in New York if he leaves Montreal on Nov. 11 at 11:10 p.m.?

   _____

   b. Vernon returns on a direct flight and saves 1 h and 45 min. When does he depart if he arrives on Nov. 18 at 1:30 a.m.?

   _____

⑯ Greta paints her room with 2 coats of paint. It takes 3 h and 10 min to apply each coat and 15 h to dry between coats. If she starts painting on Oct. 29 at 5:40 p.m., what is the earliest time she can start the 2nd coat?

   _____

⑰ Susan bought a book online on Apr. 25 at 2:35 p.m. and received it on Apr. 27 at 5:20 p.m.

   a. How long did it take for Susan's book to arrive?

   _____

   b. Susan bought another book on Apr. 29 at 11:25 a.m. When should the book arrive if the length of the delivery is expected to be the same?

   _____

ISBN: 978-1-77149-202-7

Perimeter and Area

solving a variety of word problems that involve finding the perimeter and area of shapes, including squares and rectangles

 Math Skills

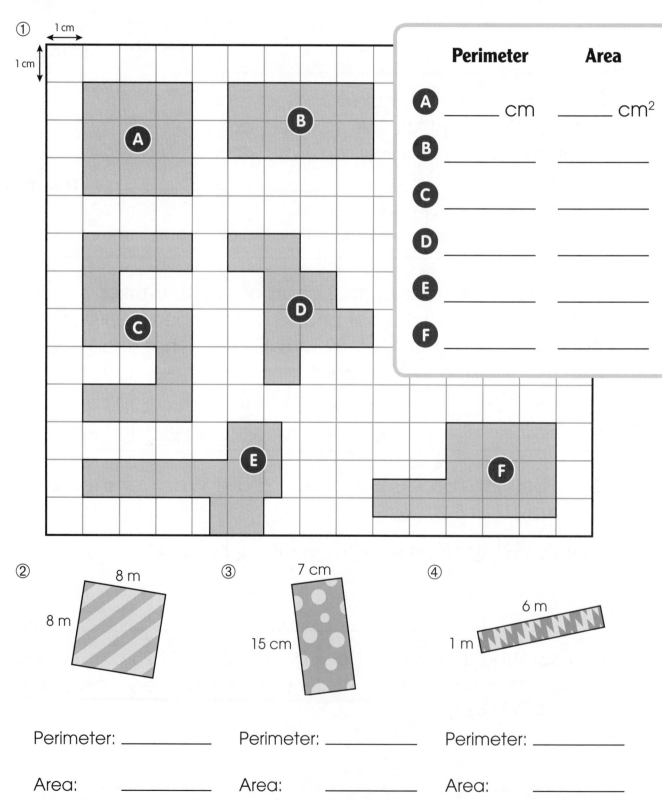

	Perimeter	Area
A	_____ cm	_____ cm²
B	_____	_____
C	_____	_____
D	_____	_____
E	_____	_____
F	_____	_____

② 8 m / 8 m

③ 7 cm / 15 cm

④ 6 m / 1 m

② Perimeter: _____

Area: _____

③ Perimeter: _____

Area: _____

④ Perimeter: _____

Area: _____

ISBN: 978-1-77149-202-7

Problem Solving

 **Try This!**

Ms. Summer wants to build a fence around her tomato garden. It has a length of 4 m and a width of 2 m. How much fencing does she need?

Solution:

Step 1: Make a sketch of the shape and label its sides.

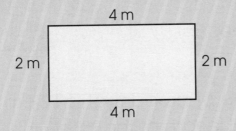

A sketch of the shape helps you visualize and understand the problem.

Step 2: Add to find the perimeter.

4 + 4 + 2 + 2 = ☐

Step 3: Write a concluding sentence.

Ms. Summer needs ☐ m of fencing.

① Macy uses a string to form a rectangle that has a length of 20 cm and a width of 15 cm. How long is the string?

The string is _____ cm long.

ISBN: 978-1-77149-202-7

② Kevin has baked 3 types of cookies and he wants to put icing on the edge of each cookie. Which cookie will need the most icing? Measure to find out.

chocolate cookie

gingerbread cookie

sesame cookie

The _____ needs the most icing.

③ Lyra cuts the crust off her slice of bread that is 12 cm long and 15 cm wide. What is the total length of the crust?

The total length of the crust is _____ cm.

④ Delilah has a 23 cm by 27 cm piece of fabric. She trims it into the largest possible square and then sews lace around it. What is the total length of the lace?

The total length of the lace is _____ cm.

ISBN: 978-1-77149-202-7

⑤

How many centimetres of framing is needed to complete the window frame?

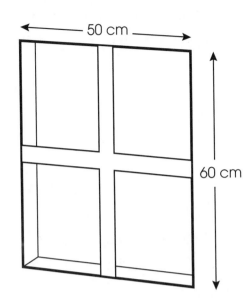

_____ cm of framing is needed.

⑥ Rafael wants to add trimming to a carpet that is 2.6 m long and 60 cm wide. How much trimming in centimetres is needed?

Tips

Remember to convert the measurements into the same units before adding.

1 cm = 10 mm
1 m = 100 cm
1 km = 1000 m

Rafael needs _____ cm of trimming.

⑦ A beach house is surrounded by a hedge that is 1450 cm long on all four sides. What is the total length of the hedge in kilometres?

The total length of the hedge is _____ km.

ISBN: 978-1-77149-202-7

⑧ The perimeter of a swimming pool is 12 000 cm. What is the width of the pool if the length is 50 m?

_____

⑨ Farmer Ben wants to build a fence around 2 side-by-side patches of land. Both patches are 100 m by 65 m and are connected on a 65-m side. How much fencing is needed for both patches of land?

_____

⑩ Lisa measured her stamps with a ruler.

    a. Lisa says, "My favourite stamp has a perimeter of 16 cm." Which is Lisa's favourite stamp?

Stamp A

_____

    b. Lisa used the stamp with the greater area on a letter. Which stamp was used?

Stamp B

_____

ISBN: 978-1-77149-202-7

⑪ A bucket of paint can cover an area of 38 m².

   a. Bob needs to paint a wall that measures 3 m by 13 m. Will one bucket of paint be enough?

_____

   b. If there is a 2 m by 1 m window on the wall, will one bucket of paint be enough?

Hints

Subtract the area of the window from the area of the wall.

_____

⑫ Thomas has a photo that measures 8 cm by 6 cm.

   a. What is the area of the photo?

_____

   b.

I have a photo frame that has an area of 49 cm² but the photo can't fit into it.

7 cm

7 cm

Explain why.

_____

_____

_____

_____

ISBN: 978-1-77149-202-7

⑬ Emily has two rectangular tablecloths, measuring 203 cm by 95 cm and 210 cm by 90 cm.

a. Emily sewed a 600-cm long fringe around the edge of one of the tablecloths. Which one did she sew the fringe onto?

_____

b. Emily used the tablecloth with a larger area for her patio table. Which one did she use?

_____

⑭ A square table has a perimeter of 320 cm. It has a pull-out that lengthens one side of the table by 30 cm.

a. What is the area of the table when the pull-out is hidden?

_____

b. What is the area of the table when it is extended with the pull-out?

Hints

The square table becomes a rectangular table when extended.

_____

⑮ Jacky wants to build a wooden frame with a strip of 12-m wood. What should the dimensions of the frame be if Jacky wants to maximize the area inside the frame?

_____

ISBN: 978-1-77149-202-7

⑯ Josh wants to combine three 25 cm by 30 cm blank canvases to make one rectangular canvas.

    a. If Josh combines the canvases by their 30-cm sides, what is the perimeter of his new canvas?

_____

    b. How much longer will the perimeter be if Josh combines the canvases by their 25-cm sides?

_____

⑰ Sally made 4 small square rugs out of a big rug. She saved the original trimming and used it to trim the 4 small rugs. How much more trimming does she need?

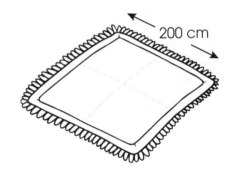

200 cm

_____

⑱ Janelle has a garden that is 5 m long and 3 m wide. She wants to extend the garden by 3 m on either the length or the width.

    a. Which side of the garden should she extend to get a bigger area?

_____

    b. How much more fencing does she need for her new garden?

_____

ISBN: 978-1-77149-202-7

Shapes and Solids

solving a variety of word problems that involve the geometric properties of shapes and solids

 Math Skills

① **Shapes**

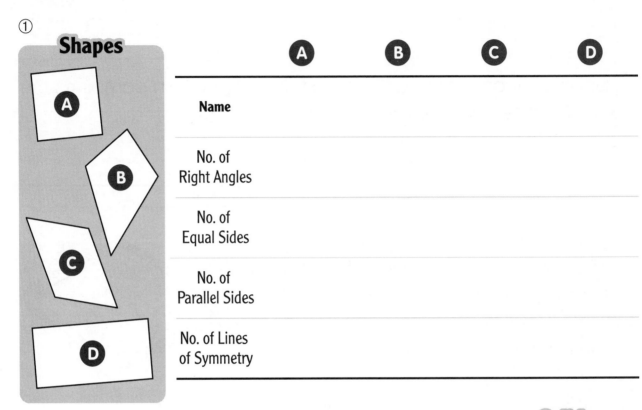

	A	B	C	D
Name				
No. of Right Angles				
No. of Equal Sides				
No. of Parallel Sides				
No. of Lines of Symmetry				

Solids

②

	E	F	G	H
Name				
No. of Faces				
No. of Vertices				
No. of Edges				

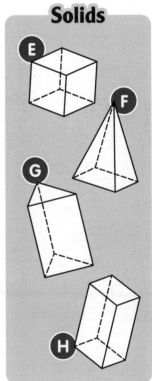

ISBN: 978-1-77149-202-7

 **Problem Solving**

Try This!

Wilson drew a square and a rectangle. He coloured the shape that had more lines of symmetry. Which shape did he colour?

Solution:

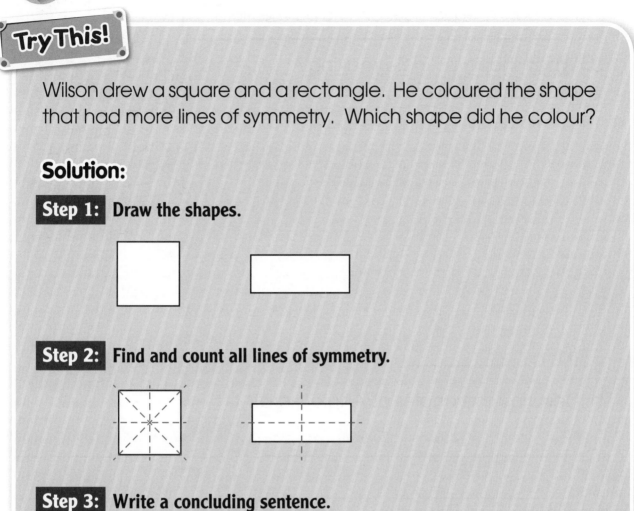

Step 1: **Draw the shapes.**

Step 2: **Find and count all lines of symmetry.**

Step 3: **Write a concluding sentence.**

Wilson coloured the ⬚ .

① Mr. Ken's handkerchief is in the shape of a quadrilateral. It has 2 pairs of parallel sides. What could be the shape(s) of the handkerchief?

The handkerchief could be in the shape of a _____

_____ .

ISBN: 978-1-77149-202-7

②

> I'm making a shape that is a quadrilateral. It has 2 pairs of equal sides and no parallel sides.

Angie

a. What shape is Angie making? Draw and name it.

It is a _____ .

b. Describe the angles of Angie's craft.

_____

_____

③ Read what the children say about the quadrilaterals.

a. Joseph says, "A trapezoid has either 2 right angles or none." Is Joseph correct? If not, how many right angles can a trapezoid have?

_____

_____

b. Joyce says, "This shape is not a quadrilateral." Is Joyce correct? Explain.

_____

_____

ISBN: 978-1-77149-202-7

④ Kyle drew 3 shapes as shown on the right.

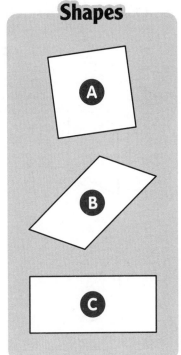

Shapes

a. Write one unique attribute of each shape that the others do not have.

Ⓐ It has _____

_____ .

Ⓑ It has _____

_____ .

Ⓒ It has _____

_____ .

b. Kyle says, "The first shape that I drew has angles that are bigger than a right angle." Name the shape.

The shape is a _____ .

⑤ Is it possible for a quadrilateral to have exactly 2 right angles? If so, draw an example and name it.

_____

ISBN: 978-1-77149-202-7

⑥ a. Draw the front, top, and side views of each solid.

Front View	**Top View**	**Side View**

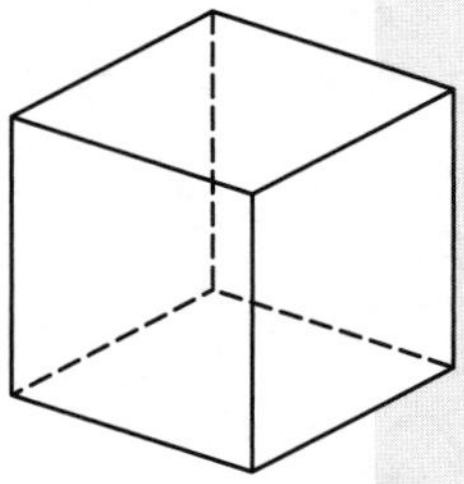

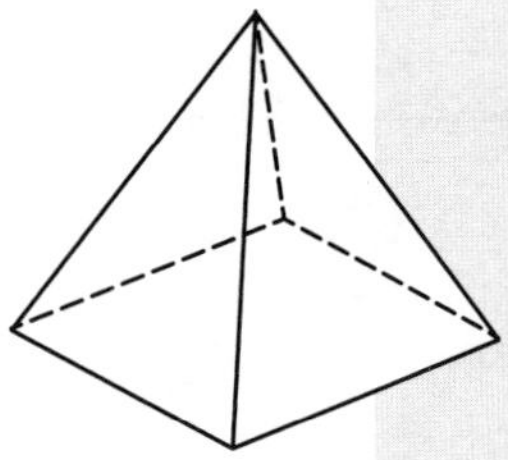

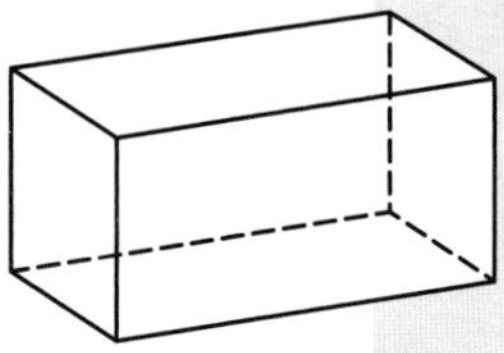

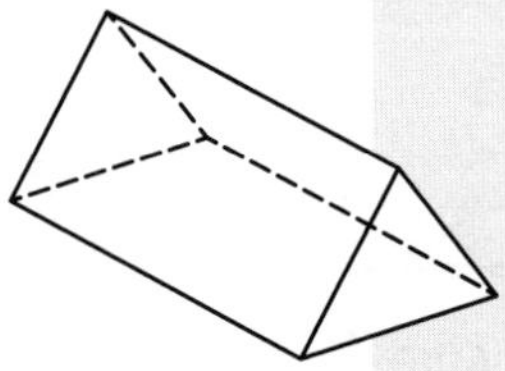

b.

Which solid's front view, top view, and side view are identical? Name it and write the number of faces, vertices, and edges that it has.

_____

_____

ISBN: 978-1-77149-202-7

⑦ Karson needs to paint a white box that is a rectangular prism. Make a sketch of the box and find the number of faces that need to be painted.

_____

⑧ Renée wants to smooth out the corners of a wooden cube. Make a sketch of the cube and find the number of corners that need to be smoothed out.

_____

⑨ Eric stacked some identical solids that can roll. Make a sketch of one of the solids and name them.

Hints

Rolling requires a round surface.

_____

⑩

I will assemble 4 pieces of triangular cardboard to make a pyramid.

Make a sketch of the pyramid and name it.

_____

⑪ The children built some solids for their science project. Name each solid and write the number of faces, vertices, and edges it has.

a. Peter's solid has 5 vertices and 1 rectangular face.

b. Zoe's solid has 6 faces that are all rectangular.

_____

_____

c. Alvin's solid has 4 vertices with triangular faces only.

d. Diana's solid has exactly 2 triangular faces and 9 edges.

_____

_____

e.

Which child's solid has no right angles on any of its faces?

_____

ISBN: 978-1-77149-202-7

⑫ Alycia made two different solids that both have triangular and rectangular faces. Name the solids. How many vertices do they have?

_____

⑬ Ernie, Francis, and Greta each draw a net that they think can fold into a cube. Which net(s) is/are correct?

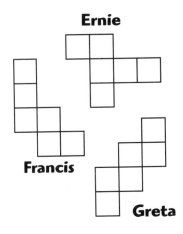

Ernie

Francis

Greta

_____

⑭ Ivan has 10 balls and 20 sticks. How many triangular pyramids can he construct?

_____

⑮ Naysha's teacher gave her this net as a template to build a 3-D figure. How many sticks does she need?

_____

⑯ Lori constructed an octagonal pyramid using sticks and balls. She then took it apart and used the sticks and balls to construct a rectangular prism. How many sticks and balls are left?

Tips

An octagon has 8 sides.

_____

ISBN: 978-1-77149-202-7

Locations and Movements

solving a variety of word problems that involve identifying transformations, locating coordinates, and performing movements

 Math Skills

① Name the transformations.

a.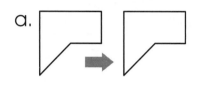

_____

b.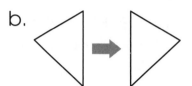

_____

c.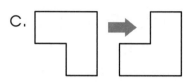

_____

d.

_____

e.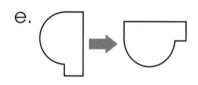

_____

f.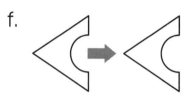

_____

② Write the coordinates.

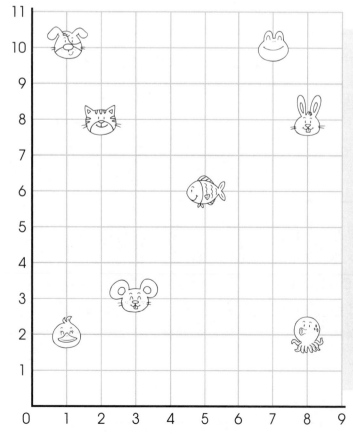

Coordinates

 ISBN: 978-1-77149-202-7

Problem Solving

Try This!

Doug the Dog wants to get the bone. How should Doug go?

Solution:

Step 1: Locate Doug and the bone. Count the number of units up from Doug.

[   ] units up

Step 2: Count the number of units to the right.

[   ] units to the right

Step 3: Write a concluding sentence.

Doug should go [   ] units up and [   ] units to the right.

① Refer to the map above.

a. How should Doug go to get the candy after getting the bone?

Doug should go _____ and _____ .

b. How should Doug go home after getting the candy?

Doug should go _____ and _____ .

② Use the map to answer the questions.

This is my neighbourhood.

Danny

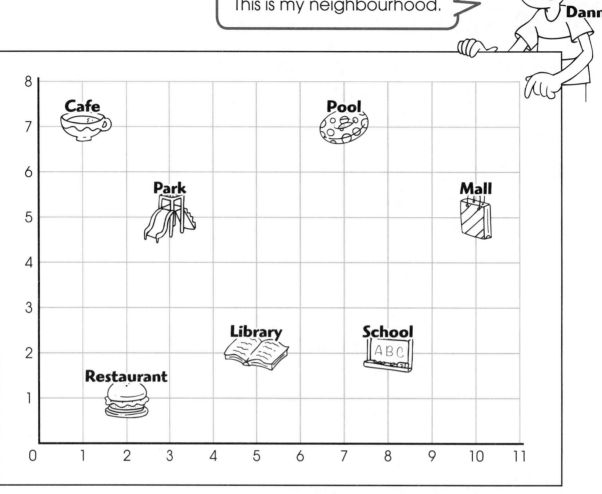

a. Write the coordinates.

- cafe _____
- park _____
- school _____

- mall _____
- pool _____
- library _____

b. Danny's house is at (7,4) and Jenny's house is at (1,2). Put a dot to locate each house and label it.

c. How should Danny go to school from home?

Danny should go _____ .

d. How should Danny go to get to the library after school?

Danny should go _____ .

ISBN: 978-1-77149-202-7

e. Danny went swimming after studying at the library. Describe Danny's route to the pool.

Danny went _____ .

f. Jenny left home and went 3 units up and 9 units to the right. Where did she go?

Jenny went to the _____ .

g. After going shopping, Jenny wanted to get a drink from either the cafe or the restaurant, whichever was closer. Which one did she go to? Describe her route.

Jenny went to the _____ by going

_____ .

h. Danny joined Jenny for a drink. How did he go after he was done swimming?

Danny went _____ .

i. Danny went home after meeting up with Jenny. He had walked 4 units to the right. Describe the rest of his route.

Danny walked _____ .

j.

> After meeting up with Danny, I took the long route home, which passes through the park.

Jenny

Describe Jenny's route.

Jenny went _____

_____ .

③ Andrew performed some transformations on the kite.

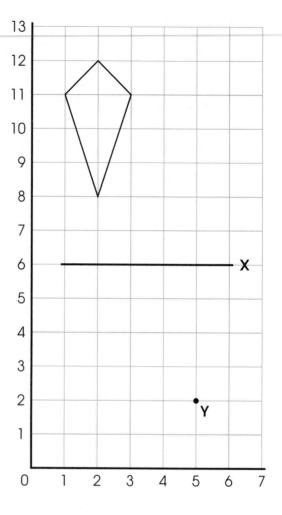

a. Draw and label the transformed images.

- Translate the kite 2 units down and 3 units to the right. Label it A.

- Reflect A over Line X. Label it B.

- Rotate B $\frac{1}{4}$ counterclockwise about Point Y. Label it C.

b. Write the coordinates of the images' vertices.

- A: _____

- B: _____

- C: _____

c. Andrew coloured one of the images. This image has (3,2) lying in it. Which image did Andrew colour?

_____

d.

> I dropped some ink and left an ink blot on (5,9). Which image has the ink blot on it?

Andrew

_____

e. Another ink blot covers all coordinates within Image B. Which coordinates are covered?

_____

ISBN: 978-1-77149-202-7

④ Helen drew half of each letter on the grid.

a. Complete the letters.

b. What are the letters?

_____

_____

c. Which letter has each pair of coordinates lying on it?

- (4,7)   _____

- (2,16)   _____

- (5,4)   _____

- (7,9)   _____

- (4,9)   _____

d. How can you transform the **L** to a **⌐**?

_____

_____

_____

e. How can you transform the **H** to an **I**?

_____

_____

_____

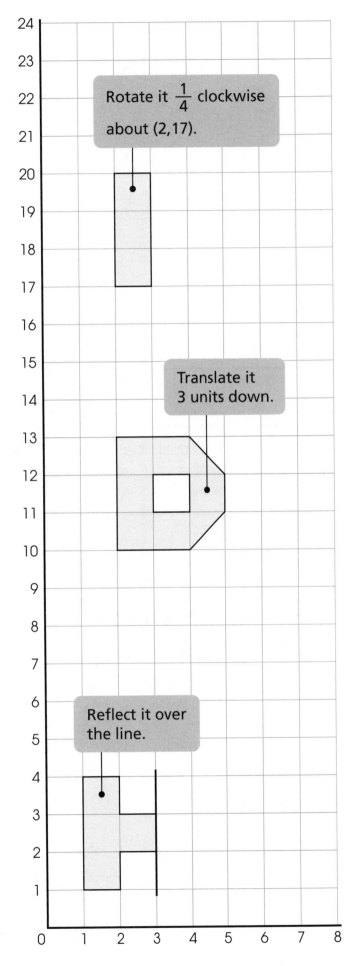

Rotate it $\frac{1}{4}$ clockwise about (2,17).

Translate it 3 units down.

Reflect it over the line.

ISBN: 978-1-77149-202-7

⑤ Kate drew Triangle A on the grid below.

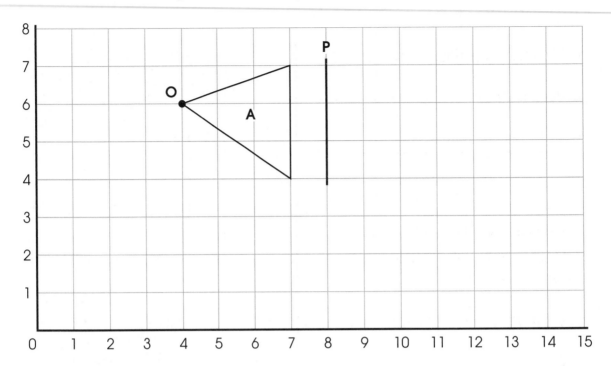

a.

Help me plot the points to draw the images. Then label them.

X: (4,6) (5,3) (2,3)

Y: (9,7) (9,4) (12,6)

Z: (11,3) (14,4) (14,1)

b. Describe the transformations.

• A to X: _____

_____

• A to Y: _____

_____

• A to Z: _____

_____

c. Kate plotted a new image by swapping the *xy* values of Image X. What are the new coordinates? Plot and draw the image.

Hints

swapping
xy values
(4,6) ⟶ (6,4)

_____

ISBN: 978-1-77149-202-7

⑥ Tyler rotated a dot $\frac{1}{2}$ clockwise about (2,2), and Rose rotated the same dot $\frac{1}{2}$ counterclockwise about (2,2).

a. Did the rotated dots have the same coordinates? Explain.

Hints

Try doing this yourself on a grid with a dot at (1,1).

_____

b. Afterwards, Tyler translated his dot 6 units up and 4 units to the right, and Rose translated hers 4 units up and 6 units to the right. How far apart are the dots horizontally and vertically?

_____

⑦ Sarah drew a triangle on a grid and is planning some transformations.

a. If the triangle is reflected over Line X, how will Point A translate?

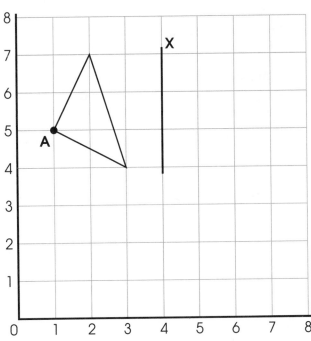

_____

b. If the triangle is rotated $\frac{3}{4}$ clockwise about (4,4), how will Point A translate?

_____

c. If the triangle is translated 4 units down and 4 units to the right, what will be the coordinates of Point A?

_____

Patterning and Equations

solving a variety of word problems that involve identifying and describing pattern rules, and writing and solving equations

Math Skills

① Complete the patterns and pattern rules.

Pattern A

2   4   8   16   _____   _____   128

Start at _____ . Multiply by _____ each time.

Pattern B

3   6   5   8   _____   10   9   _____

_____

Pattern C

5   10   9   _____   17   34   _____   _____

_____

Pattern D

4   3   9   8   _____   _____   69   _____

_____

② $6 + \heartsuit = 10$

$\heartsuit = $ _____

③ $16 - \star = 9$

$\star = $ _____

④ $3 \times \leftmoon = 15$

$\leftmoon = $ _____

⑤ $20 \div d = 5$

$d = $ _____

⑥ $a - 13 = 9 + 4$

$a = $ _____

⑦ $d + 7 = 21 - 13$

$d = $ _____

⑧ $24 \div c = 16 \div 4$

$c = $ _____

⑨ $2 \times 6 = 4 + y$

$y = $ _____

⑩ $16 \div 2 = 2 \times k$

$k = $ _____

⑪ $m + 9 = 13 \times 3$

$m = $ _____

⑫ $8 \div 2 = x + 2$

$x = $ _____

⑬ $11 - 5 = f \times 2$

$f = $ _____

ISBN: 978-1-77149-202-7

Problem Solving

Try This!

Michael made the first 4 ◣ shapes using squares. How many squares will be in the 6th ◣?

Solution:

Step 1: Find the number of squares in each ◣.

3   5   7   9

Step 2: Identify the pattern rule and extend the pattern.

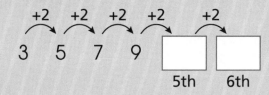

Step 3: Write a concluding sentence.

There will be ☐ squares in the 6th ◣.

① Tammy built the first 4 frames with sticks. How many sticks will there be in Frame 6?

Frame 1

Frame 2

Frame 3

Frame 4

There will be _____ sticks in Frame 6.

ISBN: 978-1-77149-202-7

② Jacob has saved $20 and he spends $3 each week. How much money will Jacob have left after 6 weeks?

Hints

Jacob spends $3 each week, so he will have $17 left after 1 week.

Jacob will have $ _____ left after 6 weeks.

③ Russell collected 2 stickers in Week 1, 3 stickers in Week 2, and 4 stickers in Week 3.

a. How many stickers did Russell collect in Week 7?

Russell collected _____ stickers in Week 7.

b. How many stickers did Russell have in total after Week 7?

Hints

The number of stickers Russell had is the sum of all the stickers collected.

Russell had _____ stickers in total after Week 7.

ISBN: 978-1-77149-202-7

④ Roy buys 1 baseball card on Day 1, sells 2 on Day 2, buys 3 on Day 3, sells 4 on Day 4, and so on.

a. What will Roy do on Day 7?

Roy will _____ on Day 7.

b. If Roy starts with 2 baseball cards, on which day will Roy run out of cards?

Roy will run out of cards on Day _____ .

⑤

I created a pattern that starts at 4, and then multiplies by 2 and subtracts by 3 each time.

What is the 6th number in the pattern?

The 6th number is _____ .

⑥ Mr. Foster made a schedule for the number of push-ups he does each day.

Mr. Foster's Schedule

Day	Number
Mon	10
Tue	12
Wed	16
Thu	24
Fri	40

a. Describe the pattern rule for the number of push-ups.

_____

b. How many push-ups will he do on Sunday?

_____

⑦ I created a schedule for the number of flowers to be planted.

Ivy

Time	Number
noon	20
1:00	24
2:00	12
3:00	16
4:00	8
5:00	
6:00	

a. How many flowers will Ivy plant at 6:00?

_____

b. If Ivy uses the same pattern rule and starts with planting 12 flowers the next day at noon, how many flowers will Ivy plant at 4:00?

_____

ISBN: 978-1-77149-202-7

⑧

We had 25 cupcakes. Some of them were sold and 12 of them remain. How many cupcakes were sold?

$25 - c = 12$

$c = \boxed{}$

Hints

Use a letter to represent an unknown.

_____

⑨ Jane has 16 pens and her sister has 11. Ken has 3 fewer pens than the total of the sisters'. How many pens does Ken have?

_____

⑩ A waiter has 56 forks to distribute. Each table seats 4 people and each person gets 2 forks. How many tables are there?

_____

⑪ Sausages come in packages of 8 and there are 11 packages in total. After putting each sausage into a bun, Ronald has 12 buns left. How many buns did Ronald start with?

_____

ISBN: 978-1-77149-202-7

⑫ Ray had 35 books on a shelf. He removed 27 books and then added back some books. If there are 42 books on the shelf, how many books did Ray add back?

_____

⑬ There were 9 packs of Popsicles in stock and 53 individual Popsicles were sold. How many Popsicles were there in each package if there are 46 Popsicles left?

_____

⑭ Stephanie planted 47 lemon seeds evenly into 5 pots. How many seeds were planted in each pot if there are 7 seeds left?

_____

⑮ Carol takes a deck of 52 cards and deals out 5 cards to each of her friends. How many friends are there if 17 cards are left in the deck?

_____

⑯

I have collected a total of 180 big and small seashells. I put every 15 small seashells into a bag. If 60 big seashells are collected, how many bags of small seashells are there?

_____

ISBN: 978-1-77149-202-7

⑰ Donna has bought a 270-piece puzzle. She organizes the pieces into edge pieces and non-edge pieces.

a. How many edge pieces are there if there are 5 times as many non-edge pieces as edge pieces?

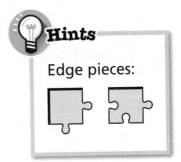

_____

b. Donna divides the non-edge pieces into 3 colours. There are 56 red pieces and 7 more blue pieces. How many green pieces are there?

_____

⑱ Lisa cuts each cheesecake into 8 equal slices and sells them individually.

a. If Lisa plans to sell 168 slices of cheesecake, how many cheesecakes should she bake?

_____

b. Lisa sells 8 slices of cheesecake in the 1st hour, 16 slices in the 2nd hour, and 24 slices in the 3rd hour. If the pattern continues, how long will it take to sell all the cheesecakes?

_____

⑲ Esme is building a tower. She used 70 straws in the 1st layer, 65 in the 2nd layer, 60 in the 3rd layer, and so on. For the 7th layer, she has already used 18 straws. How many more straws will she use to finish it?

_____

Data Management and Probability

solving a variety of word problems that involve finding the median and the mode, interpreting data from a graph, and finding probabilities

Math Skills

① Complete the bar graph with the given data.

Coin	No. of Students
nickel	12
dime	10
quarter	9
loonie	12
toonie	5

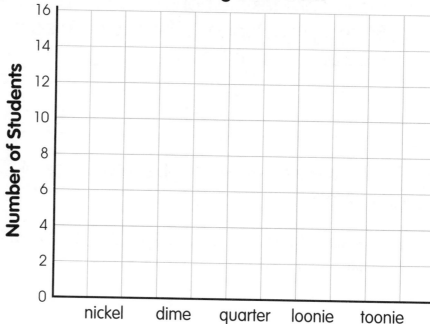

Number of Students Having Each Coin

(y-axis: Number of Students — 0, 2, 4, 6, 8, 10, 12, 14, 16)
(x-axis: Coin — nickel, dime, quarter, loonie, toonie)

② Find the probabilities.

a.

- Flip a head:

_____ out of 2

- Flip a tail:

_____

b.

- Roll a "5":

_____

- Roll a "2":

_____

c.

- Spin a "B":

_____

- Spin a "D":

_____

ISBN: 978-1-77149-202-7

Problem Solving

Refer to the bar graph on page 104. Find the median and the mode.

Solution:

Step 1: Put the numbers in order from least to greatest.

5   9   10   12   12

Step 2: Find the median and the mode.

5   9   **10**   **12**   **12**
median   mode

The median is the middle number in an ordered set of data. The mode is the number that appears most often.

Step 3: Write a concluding sentence.

The median is ☐ and the

mode is ☐ .

① Betty surveyed her friends' shoe sizes. What are the median and the mode?

Shoe Sizes

7	5	6
5	6	5
5	4	7

The median is _____ and the mode is _____ .

② Complete the bar graph and answer the questions.

Number of Rainy Days in May in 6 Cities

City	Toronto	Hamilton	London	Ottawa	Barrie	Waterloo
No. of Days	14	11	16	18	12	12

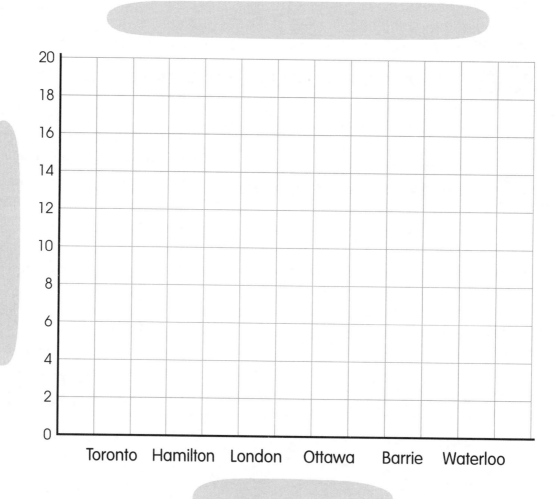

a. Which city has the

• most rainy days?

• fewest rainy days?

_____

_____

b. Which city has

• 20 non-rainy days?

• 13 non-rainy days?

_____

_____

ISBN: 978-1-77149-202-7

c. What is the median number of rainy days?

Hints

When there is an even number of values, add the 2 middle values and then divide by 2 to find the median.

The median is _____ .

d. What is the mode number of rainy days? Name the cities.

The mode is _____ and the cities are _____ .

e. Are the cities that have the mode number of non-rainy days the same as those that have the mode number of rainy days?

_____

f.

> The city that we live in has the smallest difference between the number of rainy days and the number of non-rainy days.

Name the city.

The city is _____ .

③ Leslie has opened a lemonade stand and he recorded the sales in July on the calendar.

a. What is the median sales on

- Wednesdays?

_____

- Fridays?

_____

JULY						
Sun	Mon	Tue	Wed	Thu	Fri	Sat
		$19	$13	$12	$12	$24
$25	$5	$11	$10	$15	$9	$24
$21	$8	$7	$14	$10	$15	$28
$22	$8	$10	$6	$17	$14	$19
$22	$9	$13	$7	$11		

b. Complete the chart that shows the total sales for each day of the week. Then make a horizontal bar graph.

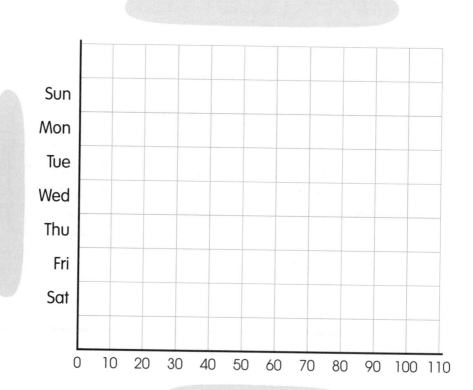

Day	Total Sales
Sun	
Mon	
Tue	
Wed	
Thu	
Fri	
Sat	

ISBN: 978-1-77149-202-7

c. Which day of the week has the

- most sales?

- least sales?

_____   _____

d. The total sales is greater on Tuesdays than on Fridays. Does that mean lemonade sells better on a Tuesday than on a Friday? Explain.

_____

_____

_____

e. If Leslie continues his lemonade stand in August, how likely is it that total sales on Mondays will exceed total sales on Sundays?

_____

f.

I buy a cup of lemonade once a week.

What is the probability that he will get a cup of lemonade on

- Tuesday?

_____

- Monday or Friday?

_____

- a weekday?

_____

- the weekend?

_____

④ This dice is labelled 1 to 6. I will roll it once.

Tom

a. What is the probability of rolling

- an even number?

_____

- a number less than 4?

_____

💡 **Hints**

The number 4 is not included.

- a number that is not 5?

_____

_____

b. Which is more likely,

- rolling a 3 or a number greater than 3?

_____

_____

- rolling a number greater than 1 or a number less than 2?

_____

_____

c. An 8-sided dice is labelled 1 to 8. Would the probability of rolling a 1 be greater or less than Tom's dice?

_____

ISBN: 978-1-77149-202-7

⑤

> I'm going to flip a coin twice. Complete the tree diagram to show all the possible outcomes.

1st Flip	2nd Flip	Outcome

H

T

a. How many possible outcomes are there?

_____

b. What are the possible outcomes?

_____

c. What is the probability of

• flipping 2 heads?

_____

• flipping at least 1 tail?

_____

d. What are the probabilities of flipping 2 tails, and flipping a head and a tail? Which is more likely?

_____

ISBN: 978-1-77149-202-7

ISBN: 978-1-77149-202-7

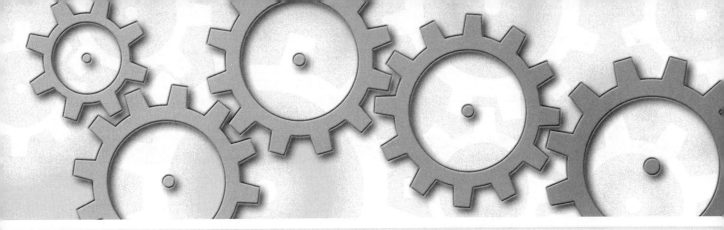

Section 2:
Critical-thinking Questions

Students are required to solve multi-step questions which involve various topics in each.

Topics Covered

	Number Sense and Numeration	Measurement	Geometry and Spatial Sense	Patterning and Algebra	Data Management and Probability	My Record ✔ correct ✘ incorrect
1	addition multiplication					
2	decimals	perimeter				
3	addition	time				
4	multiplication division					
5		perimeter	shapes solids			
6		time	movements			
7	addition	area		patterning		
8	fractions decimals					
9	division	perimeter area				
10	division	area				
11	decimals			patterning		
12	multiplication money	area				
13	division decimals	perimeter	shapes			
14	money	time				
15	decimals			patterning	data management	
16		time	locations movements			
17	decimals	perimeter	movements			
18		perimeter area	solids			
19	fractions				data management	
20			shapes		probability	

ISBN: 978-1-77149-202-7

① Each jar of fruit punch contains 540 mL of apple juice and 280 mL of orange juice. How much juice is there in 5 jars?

Juice in 1 jar: _____ + _____

= _____

Juice in 5 jars: _____ × _____

= _____

There is _____ of juice in 5 jars.

② A quadrilateral has a perimeter of 8 cm. The lengths of three of its sides are shorter than 1.6 cm. What is the length of the 4th side?

Hints

This question has more than one answer.

③ A movie theatre earns $1623 for each movie shown. If a movie is 2 h 30 min long, how much will the theatre earn at most from 3 p.m. to 10 p.m.?

Topics covered:

Question 1
- addition
- multiplication

Question 2
- decimals
- perimeter

Question 3
- addition
- time

ISBN: 978-1-77149-202-7

④ Bosco has 18 trays of 16 brownies. He wants to package them into bags of 9 brownies. How many bags does he need?

⑤ Each face of a cube has a perimeter of 252 cm. What is the total length of all the edges of the cube?

Hints

The faces of a cube are the same.

⑥ Elle is walking home. If she walks 200 m in 3 min, how much time does it take her to get home?

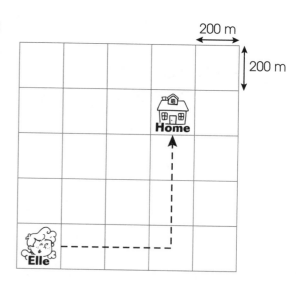

Topics covered:

Question 4
• multiplication
• division

Question 5
• perimeter
• shapes
• solids

Question 6
• time
• movements

ISBN: 978-1-77149-202-7

⑦ Jerry draws a series of squares with increasing side lengths, starting at 30 cm and increasing by 20 cm for each square. What is the total area of the first 3 squares?

⑧ Adeline ate 0.6 of a box of chocolate and Janice ate 0.2 of it. How much of the box of chocolate is left? Write your answer as a fraction.

⑨ A piece of square cardboard has a perimeter of 168 cm. Tiffany cuts it in half to make 2 identical rectangles. What is the area of each rectangle?

Hints

Make a sketch of the shapes first.

⑩ Refer to Question 9. If Tiffany cuts one of the rectangles into squares with side lengths of 3 cm, how many squares will she make?

Topics covered:

Question 7	**Question 8**	**Question 9**	**Question 10**
• addition	• fractions	• division	• division
• area	• decimals	• perimeter	• area
• patterning		• area	

ISBN: 978-1-77149-202-7

⑪ Blake ran a 5-km race in 2011, a 5.5-km race in 2012, and a 6-km race in 2013. How many kilometres had Blake run by the end of 2015 if the pattern continued?

Hints

Use a table to record the distance each year.

⑫ A piece of fabric costs $12 for every square metre. Liam has 13 $20 bills and 7 $5 bills. How much will he have left if he buys a piece of fabric that measures 12 m by 2 m?

⑬ A playground is in the shape of a parallelogram. The fence that surrounds it is 183 m and one of its sides is 40.5 m. What are the lengths of the other 3 sides?

Hints

A parallelogram has 2 pairs of equal sides.

Topics covered:

Question 11	**Question 12**	**Question 13**
• decimals	• multiplication	• division
• patterning	• money	• decimals
	• area	• perimeter
		• shapes

ISBN: 978-1-77149-202-7

⑭ A parking meter costs $0.25 for every 6 minutes. Artie inserts 2 loonies, 1 quarter, and 5 nickels into the meter to park from 1:32 p.m. to 2:44 p.m. How much more money is needed?

⑮ Sandra runs 2.7 km on Day 1. Afterwards, she will run 0.6 km more than the previous day. What is the median distance that she runs in the first week?

⑯ A car is located at (2,4). Every 3 minutes, it moves 3 units to the right and 2 units up. What will the car's location be after 45 minutes?

Topics covered:

Question 14	**Question 15**	**Question 16**
• money	• decimals	• time
• time	• patterning	• locations
	• data management	• movements

ISBN: 978-1-77149-202-7

⑰ The image shows half of a stamp. Mona completes it by drawing its reflection. What is the perimeter of the stamp?

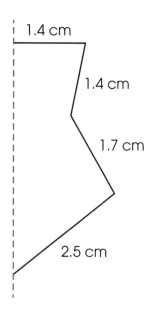

1.4 cm

1.4 cm

1.7 cm

2.5 cm

⑱ A rectangular prism with the dimensions of 21 cm by 18 cm by 4 cm is unfolded into its net as shown below. What is the perimeter and area of the net?

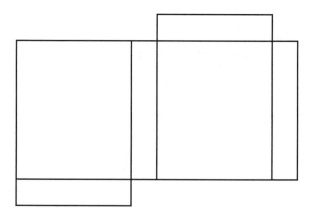

Topics covered:

Question 17	**Question 18**
• decimals	• perimeter
• perimeter	• area
• movements	• solids

ISBN: 978-1-77149-202-7

⑲ Brendon counted the number of letters each word has in a poem and recorded the result in a graph. What fraction of the words have the median number of letters?

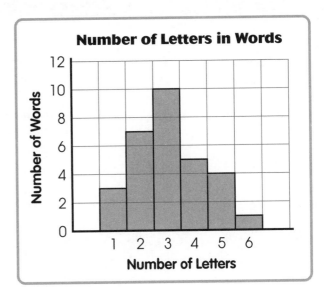

Number of Letters in Words

⑳ Rosa puts a square, a rectangle, a parallelogram, a rhombus, a trapezoid, and a kite into a bag and randomly picks one. Is she more likely to pick a shape with more than 1 line of symmetry or a shape with at least 1 pair of parallel sides?

**Hints**

Organize the properties of the shapes in a table. Then find the probabilities.

Topics covered:

Question 19
- fractions
- data management

Question 20
- shapes
- probability

ISBN: 978-1-77149-202-7

Students are required to solve multi-step questions which involve various topics in each.

Topics Covered

	Number Sense and Numeration	Measurement	Geometry and Spatial Sense	Patterning and Algebra	Data Management and Probability	My Record ✔ correct ✘ incorrect
1	money	time				
2	money		solids			
3	multiplication	perimeter				
4	fractions				data management	
5					probability / data management	
6	multiplication division			equations		
7			locations movements	patterning		
8		perimeter area	movements			
9	decimals		shapes	patterning		
10	division fractions					
11			solids	patterning		
12	multiplication	perimeter	solids			
13				patterning	data management	
14		area		patterning		
15	multiplication decimals	time				
16	division	perimeter area				
17	fractions	time				
18	fractions	perimeter				
19	division			equations	data management	
20				patterning	probability	

ISBN: 978-1-77149-202-7

① Chris buys 2 cookies every day. 1 cookie costs $1.50. After one week, how much will Chris spend on cookies?

Cost in 1 day: _____ + _____

= _____

Cost in 1 week: _____ × _____

= _____

Chris will spend _____ on cookies.

② Joel has 2 $5 bills, 3 toonies, and 1 loonie. He wants to buy square boards to make cubes. If each board costs 50 cents, how many cubes can he afford to make?

③ Alexis wants to build a fence. One metre of fencing costs $32. How much will it cost Alexis to build her fence?

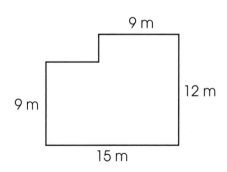

9 m

12 m

9 m

15 m

Topics covered:

Question 1	Question 2	Question 3
• money	• money	• multiplication
• time	• solids	• perimeter

ISBN: 978-1-77149-202-7

④ Tyler conducted a survey on his friends' favourite hobbies. He recorded the results in a bar graph. What fraction of his friends chose singing?

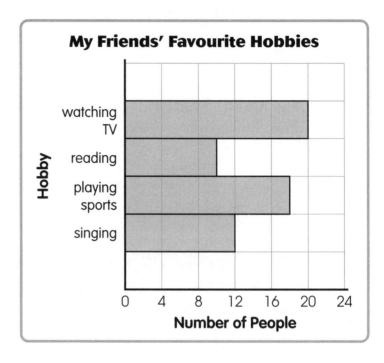

⑤ Refer to Question 4. If a person is picked at random, what is the probability that the person's favourite hobby is either watching TV or playing sports?

Topics covered:

Question 4
- fractions
- data management

Question 5
- probability
- data management

ISBN: 978-1-77149-202-7

⑥ Leo prepares 8 pieces of dough which make exactly 24 dozen doughnuts. Write an equation to find the number of doughnuts that 1 piece of dough makes.

⑦ Look at the stars. Write the pattern rule and the coordinates of the next 2 stars.

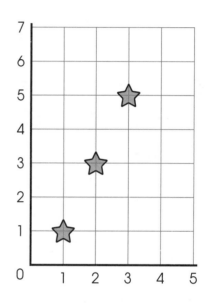

⑧ A rectangular pamphlet is folded in half. The perimeter of the pamphlet is 42 cm when folded and 54 cm when unfolded. What is the area of the pamphlet when unfolded?

 **Hints**

Draw a diagram to see what changes when the pamphlet is unfolded.

Topics covered:

Question 6	**Question 7**	**Question 8**
• multiplication	• locations	• perimeter
• division	• movements	• area
• equations	• patterning	• movements

⑨ The table records the side lengths of regular shapes. Follow the pattern to find the perimeter of a regular octagon.

Side Lengths of Regular Shapes

Shape	Side Length (cm)
triangle	2.5
square	3
pentagon	3.5

⑩ A piece of string is 45 m long. Dave uses $\frac{2}{3}$ of it to make 3-m and/or 4-m pieces. How many 3-m and 4-m pieces can there be?

Hints

This question has more than one answer.

⑪ Ryan constructs a series of solids using 1-cm³ cubes. How many 1-cm³ cubes are needed for the next solid in the series? Draw it.

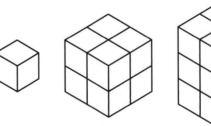
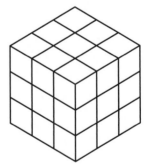

Topics covered:

Question 9	**Question 10**	**Question 11**
• decimals	• division	• solids
• shapes	• fractions	• patterning
• patterning		

ISBN: 978-1-77149-202-7

⑫ Elizabeth draws a net for a cube with a side length of 22 mm. What is the perimeter of the net in centimetres?

Hints

There is only one answer.

⑬ The amount of sand flowing down an hourglass is shown in the graph. If the pattern continues, how long will it take for all the sand to flow down?

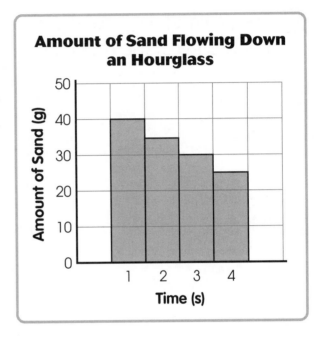

Amount of Sand Flowing Down an Hourglass

⑭ Rey draws figures in a pattern. What is the area of the 6th figure?

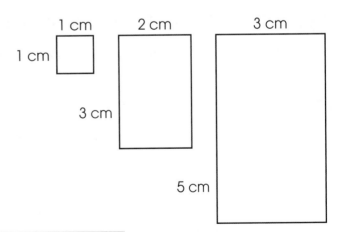

Topics covered:

Question 12	**Question 13**	**Question 14**
• multiplication	• patterning	• area
• perimeter	• data management	• patterning
• solids		

ISBN: 978-1-77149-202-7

⑮ Florence practises the violin for 0.5 hour each day. How many minutes does she practise the violin in 21 days?

⑯ The perimeter of the square is 784 cm. What is the area of the shaded part?

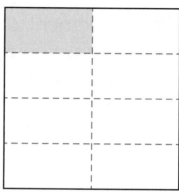

⑰ It is 6:37 p.m. What was the time $2\frac{2}{3}$ hours ago?

⑱ Johnny has 20 1-cm² square tiles. He uses $\frac{1}{4}$ of them to make a rectangle. What is the perimeter of the rectangle?

Topics covered:

Question 15	**Question 16**	**Question 17**	**Question 18**
• multiplication	• division	• fractions	• fractions
• decimals	• perimeter	• time	• perimeter
• time	• area		

ISBN: 978-1-77149-202-7

⑲ Sally surveyed 85 people and graphed the results in a bar graph. However, she forgot to include the scale. Write an equation to find the interval of the scale. Then add the scale to the graph.

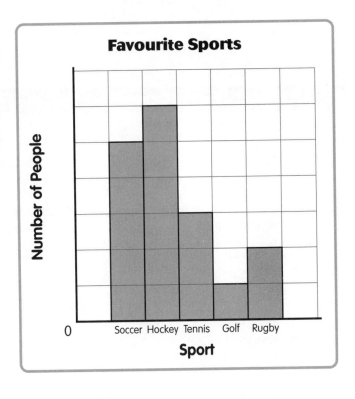

Favourite Sports

Number of People

0   Soccer Hockey Tennis Golf Rugby

Sport

⑳ Every day, Ashley records the number of marbles that she has in her collection. On Day 7, there are 3 red marbles. If she picks a marble randomly, what is the probability that she will pick a red marble?

Ashley's Marble Collection

Day	No. of ◎
1	4
2	5
3	7
4	11

Topics covered:

Question 19
- division
- equations
- data management

Question 20
- patterning
- probability

ISBN: 978-1-77149-202-7

Students are required to solve multi-step questions which involve various topics in each.

ISBN: 978-1-77149-202-7

Topics Covered

	Number Sense and Numeration	Measurement	Geometry and Spatial Sense	Patterning and Algebra	Data Management and Probability
1	subtraction division	time			
2	fractions		movements		
3	multiplication decimals	area			
4	multiplication fractions				
5	addition multiplication		solids		
6	decimals			patterning	
7	multiplication	time			
8	fractions				data management
9	decimals		locations movements		
10		perimeter area		equations	
11	money	time			
12	multiplication	time			
13	money			patterning	
14		area	movements		
15		time		patterning	
16			solids	patterning	
17	fractions		shapes	equations	
18	fractions	area			
19	fractions				probability
20			solids		data management

My Record

✔ correct
✘ incorrect

① A barrel had 4709 mL of water. It had leaked for four hours until there was only 1245 mL of water left. How much water did it leak every 30 minutes?

Amount of water leaked : _____ - _____

= _____

Amount of water leaked every 30 minutes : _____ ÷ _____
↑
no. of 30-minute intervals in 4 hours

= _____

The barrel leaked _____ of water every 30 minutes.

② Cassie places a mirror along the bottom edge of her name tag. What fraction of the letters in the mirror are the same as the original?

③ Henry's painting is 17 cm by 32 cm. He wants to build a 1.5-cm thick frame around it. What will the area of the frame be?

 **Hints**

Draw a diagram. The area of the frame excludes the painting's area.

Topics covered:

Question 1
- subtraction
- division
- time

Question 2
- fractions
- movements

Question 3
- multiplication
- decimals
- area

ISBN: 978-1-77149-202-7

④ A package has 30 tea bags. $\frac{2}{5}$ of them are Earl Grey. How many Earl Grey tea bags are there in 58 packages?

⑤ How many wooden triangles are needed to build 109 triangular pyramids and 176 triangular prisms?

⑥ The gas price was 89.9¢ for each litre in Week 1, 90.2¢ in Week 2, and 90.5¢ in Week 3. What will the gas price be in Week 5 if the pattern continues?

⑦ A helicopter left at 11:20 a.m. and arrived at 1:50 p.m. The helicopter used 50 L of gas each hour. How much gas did it use for the flight?

Topics covered:

Question 4	**Question 5**	**Question 6**	**Question 7**
• multiplication	• addition	• decimals	• multiplication
• fractions	• multiplication	• patterning	• time
	• solids		

ISBN: 978-1-77149-202-7

⑧ Look at the bar graph. Which music genre has $\frac{3}{4}$ of the number of votes for pop music? How many children voted for this music genre?

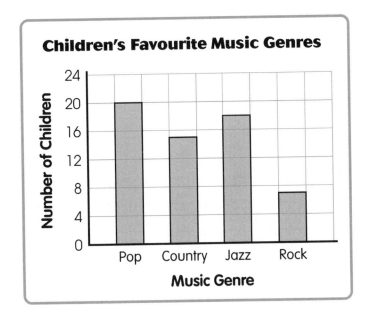

⑨ The library is 6 km away from home and 3 km from school. Give one pair of possible coordinates for the library.

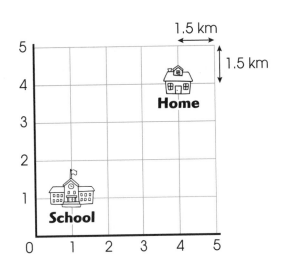

Topics covered:

Question 8
- fractions
- data management

Question 9
- decimals
- locations
- movements

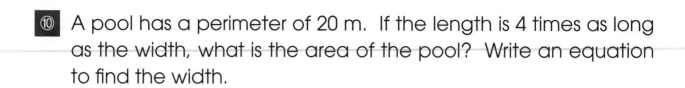

⑩ A pool has a perimeter of 20 m. If the length is 4 times as long as the width, what is the area of the pool? Write an equation to find the width.

⑪ A long distance phone call costs $1.75 for the first 5 minutes, and 50¢ for each additional minute after. How long was Katie's phone call if she paid $6.75?

⑫ It takes Candace 1 hour and 15 minutes to read 3 chapters of her book. Her book has 12 chapters. How many minutes will it take her to read the entire book?

Topics covered:

Question 10	**Question 11**	**Question 12**
• perimeter	• money	• multiplication
• area	• time	• time
• equations		

ISBN: 978-1-77149-202-7

⑬ Ali followed a pattern to arrange his coins into rows. He traded the coins in the 8th row for the fewest coins. Which coins did he get?

Row 1

Row 2

Row 3

⑭ Peter slides his stamp 8 cm to the left and 5 cm up on a page. What is the area of the shape created by the stamp in mm²?

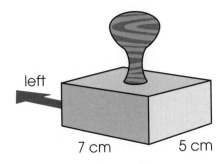

left

7 cm   5 cm

⑮ Jeremy runs for 15 min 30 s on Monday, 18 min 5 s on Tuesday, and 20 min 40 s on Wednesday. If the pattern continues, how long will he run on Friday?

Topics covered:

Question 13
• money
• patterning

Question 14
• area
• movements

Question 15
• time
• patterning

ISBN: 978-1-77149-202-7

⑯ There is a relationship between the number of vertices in a prism and the number of sides its base has. Describe the relationship. How many vertices does a nonagonal prism have?

Tips

A nonagon has 9 sides.

⑰ Miranda used 87 sticks to make rhombuses and triangles. 15 of the shapes were rhombuses. Write an equation to find the number of triangles. What fraction of the shapes were triangles?

⑱ A square bulletin board has a side length of 60 cm. A poster takes up $\frac{1}{6}$ of the bulletin board. What are the area and dimensions of the poster?

Hints

This question has more than one answer.

Topics covered:

Question 16	**Question 17**	**Question 18**
• solids	• fractions	• fractions
• patterning	• shapes	• area
	• equations	

ISBN: 978-1-77149-202-7

⑲ On Spinner A, $\frac{1}{2}$ is red, $\frac{1}{4}$ is green, and the rest is blue. On Spinner B, $\frac{1}{6}$ is red, $\frac{1}{3}$ is yellow, and the rest is blue. On which spinner will it be more likely to spin blue? What is the probability?

Tips

Draw the spinners to help you find the answer.

⑳ Leslie created a bar graph to show the number of edges different pyramids have. Identify and describe the 3 mistakes that she made. Make the corrections in the graph.

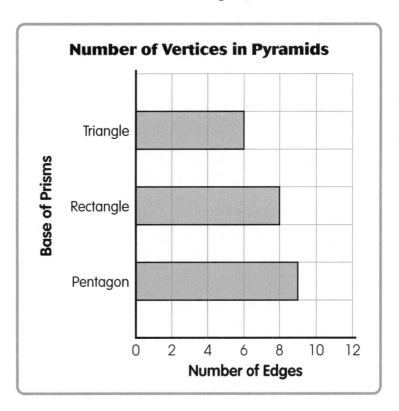

Number of Vertices in Pyramids

Topics covered:

Question 19
- fractions
- probability

Question 20
- solids
- data management

ISBN: 978-1-77149-202-7

4

Students are required to solve multi-step questions which involve various topics in each.

Topics Covered

	Number Sense and Numeration	Measurement	Geometry and Spatial Sense	Patterning and Algebra	Data Management and Probability	My Record ✔ correct ✘ incorrect
1	multiplication	perimeter				☐
2	multiplication		shapes			☐
3			movements		probability	☐
4	decimals money					☐
5	fractions decimals					☐
6	addition fractions					☐
7	multiplication	area				☐
8	money				data management	☐
9	division		locations movements			☐
10	money			patterning		☐
11	division	time				☐
12	division	area				☐
13	fractions	time		patterning		☐
14	decimals		solids			☐
15	division fractions	area				☐
16	division	time	shapes			☐
17	multiplication division					☐
18	division			equations		☐
19		time		patterning	data management	☐
20	division money				probability	☐

ISBN: 978-1-77149-202-7

① Abel's backyard has dimensions of 442 cm by 558 cm. He wants to build fencing all around it. How much will the fencing cost if each metre costs $145?

Perimeter of backyard: _____ + _____ + _____ + _____

= _____

Cost of fencing: _____ × _____

= _____   ↑
              perimeter of backyard in metres

The fencing will cost _____ .

② A banquet hall has 142 square tables, 63 pentagonal tables, and 37 hexagonal tables. Each side of a table seats 1 guest. How many guests can the banquet hall seat?

③ Rotate the word "HORIZON" 180°. Write the rotated word in the box.

A rotated letter is picked from the box. What is the probability that the rotated letter is the same as its original?

— Rotated Word —

Topics covered:

Question 1
- multiplication
- perimeter

Question 2
- multiplication
- shapes

Question 3
- movements
- probability

ISBN: 978-1-77149-202-7

④ The thickness of a loonie and a quarter is about 1.9 mm and 1.6 mm respectively. If Sandra stacks $2.50 in loonies and quarters, what is the stack's shortest possible height in centimetres?

⑤ A baker had 1 cup of sugar. He used 0.65 of the sugar to make brownies. What fraction of the sugar is left?

⑥ 1833 adults and 1167 children attended a hockey game. $\frac{2}{5}$ of the attendees wore jerseys. If 325 children wore jerseys, how many adults wore jerseys?

⑦ A countertop is covered with 73 tiles that are 8 cm by 6 cm each. What is the area of the countertop?

Topics covered:

Question 4	**Question 5**	**Question 6**	**Question 7**
• decimals	• fractions	• addition	• multiplication
• money	• decimals	• fractions	• area

ISBN: 978-1-77149-202-7

⑧ Leo's savings are shown in the bar graph. He buys a $4.85 toy car using all his quarters. If Leo gets his change back in the fewest coins, how many nickels and dimes will he have?

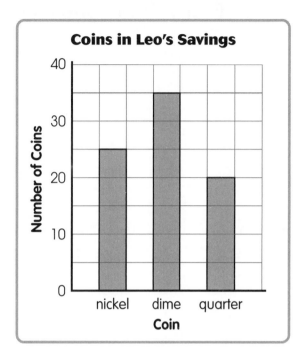

⑨ John starts jogging at (4,3). He jogs 300 m to the left, 400 m up, 200 m to the right, and then 500 m down. Draw to show his route.

A park is at (3,2). Is John at the park now?

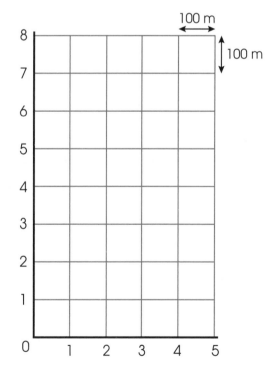

Topics covered:

Question 8
- money
- data management

Question 9
- division
- locations
- movements

ISBN: 978-1-77149-202-7

⑩ Bethany has $1.75. She earns 1 quarter and 2 nickels on Monday, 3 quarters and 4 nickels on Tuesday, and 5 quarters and 6 nickels on Wednesday. How much will she have in total on Friday if the pattern continues?

⑪ A novel has 104 pages. Jordan reads 8 pages in 15 minutes. If he starts reading at 9:30 a.m., what time will he finish reading the novel?

⑫ Mr. Lee wants to add a backsplash that has an area of 0.54 m². The backsplash is covered by square tiles that have a side length of 3 cm. How many tiles are needed?

Hints

0.54 m² = 5400 cm²

Topics covered:

Question 10	**Question 11**	**Question 12**
• money	• division	• division
• patterning	• time	• area

ISBN: 978-1-77149-202-7

⑬ Harper has a pencil that is 18 cm long. It becomes 2 cm shorter every 3 days. If today is March 13, on which day will the pencil be $\frac{1}{3}$ of its original length?

⑭ Sylvester builds a square-based prism using the net. He strengthens the prism by gluing sticks on the edges of the solid. How many sticks does he need? What are their lengths?

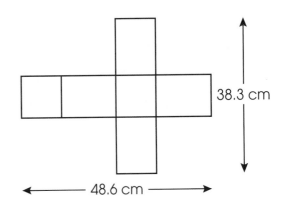

38.3 cm

48.6 cm

⑮ Daniel made a piece of biscuit dough that measured 40 cm by 40 cm. He cut the dough into 100 squares and baked them. The baked biscuits are $\frac{1}{4}$ bigger than their original size. What is the area of each baked biscuit?

Topics covered:

Question 13
• fractions
• time
• patterning

Question 14
• decimals
• solids

Question 15
• division
• fractions
• area

ISBN: 978-1-77149-202-7

A snail travels 216 cm in one hour. If it takes the snail 30 minutes to complete a lap around an equilateral triangle, how long is one side of the triangle?

An equilateral triangle has 3 equal sides.

⑰ 11 classes are going on a field trip. Each class has 19 students. They will travel in 5 buses. How many students will be on each bus if they are split among the buses as evenly as possible?

⑱ For a school concert, a student ticket cost $3 and an adult ticket cost $5. The number of both tickets sold were the same. How many tickets were sold if $1568 was made? Write an equation to find the answer.

Topics covered:

Question 16
- division
- time
- shapes

Question 17
- multiplication
- division

Question 18
- division
- equations

ISBN: 978-1-77149-202-7

⑲ The bar graph shows how much time Jimmy spends on exercising each week. If the pattern continues, how many more minutes will Jimmy exercise in Week 6 than in Week 1?

⑳ George has $20 in loonies, quarters, dimes, and nickels. He has $5 in each type of coin. If he loses one of the coins, what is the probability that it is a quarter?

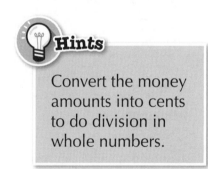

Hints

Convert the money amounts into cents to do division in whole numbers.

Topics covered:

Question 19	**Question 20**
• time	• division
• patterning	• money
• data management	• probability

ISBN: 978-1-77149-202-7

Students are required to solve multi-step questions which involve various topics in each.

Topics Covered

	Number Sense and Numeration	Measurement	Geometry and Spatial Sense	Patterning and Algebra	Data Management and Probability	My Record ✔ correct ✗ incorrect
1	subtraction fractions					
2	division	perimeter				
3	multiplication			equations		
4	multiplication	area	solids			
5	money				probability	
6	fractions decimals	time				
7	fractions decimals					
8	decimals				data management	
9	division	perimeter	shapes			
10	money	time				
11	fractions	time		patterning		
12	decimals		movements			
13	subtraction multiplication					
14	multiplication	area			data management	
15		perimeter area			data management	
16			solids		probability	
17	decimals	perimeter	shapes			
18		perimeter	shapes	patterning		
19	decimals		locations movements			
20	multiplication division	area				

ISBN: 978-1-77149-202-7

① There are 2000 hats in a hat store. $\frac{3}{4}$ of the hats are baseball caps. If 1094 baseball caps are sold, how many are left?

No. of baseball caps: $\frac{3}{4}$ of 2000 is _____ . ⟵ $\frac{3}{4} = \dfrac{}{2000}$ × 500

No. of baseball caps left: _____ – _____

= _____

_____ are left.

② A toy train travels 2 m every second on its rectangular track. The dimensions of the track are 4500 cm and 2500 cm. How many seconds will it take the train to travel 2 laps?

Hints

Convert the measurements from "cm" to "m" first.

③ Luke recorded the number of balls he scored for each point value in skee ball. His total score was 730. Write an equation to find how many 10-point balls he scored.

Luke's Results of Each Ball

Points for Each Ball	No. of Balls
10	?
20	15
30	12
40	0
50	1

Topics covered:

Question 1	**Question 2**	**Question 3**
• subtraction	• division	• multiplication
• fractions	• perimeter	• equations

ISBN: 978-1-77149-202-7

④ A large cube is painted. It is cut into 27 small cubes as shown. How many small cubes have 729 cm² painted?

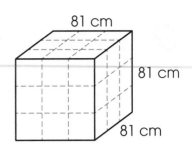

81 cm

81 cm

81 cm

⑤ Jenny inserts a toonie into a vending machine to buy a $1.65 pack of gum. If the vending machine dispenses change at random, what is the probability that Jenny will get at least 1 dime in change?

⑥ Charles filmed 3 videos. Their lengths were 1.5 minutes, 2 minutes 26 seconds, and $6\frac{4}{5}$ minutes. He merged the videos and cut 126 seconds from it. What was the final length of the video?

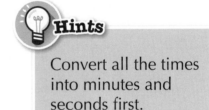

Hints

Convert all the times into minutes and seconds first.

Topics covered:

Question 4	**Question 5**	**Question 6**
• multiplication	• money	• fractions
• area	• probability	• decimals
• solids		• time

ISBN: 978-1-77149-202-7

⑦ A pizza is divided into 8 slices and each slice is sold for $3.80. How much does $\frac{1}{2}$ of the pizza cost?

⑧ Tyler has 5 books that are 31.2 cm tall when stacked together. The median thickness is 6.7 cm and the mode thickness is 5.4 cm. How thick is the thickest book?

Hints

The thicknesses of all the books are in one decimal place.

⑨ Ray wants to rearrange the fences on his square farm. The old design used 216 m of fencing. How much more fencing is needed for the new design?

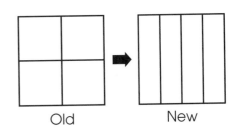

Old   New

⑩ Lily receives an allowance of 1 toonie, 3 dimes, and 3 nickels every Saturday. If May 1 was a Friday, how much did Lily receive in total in May?

Topics covered:

Question 7	**Question 8**	**Question 9**	**Question 10**
• fractions	• decimals	• division	• money
• decimals	• data management	• perimeter	• time
		• shapes	

⑪ Carlos plays video games for $3\frac{1}{3}$ hours on Monday. His parents tell him to cut the amount of time he plays in half each day. How long will he play video games on Thursday?

Hints

Convert the time from hours to minutes first.

⑫ Matt has left home for work. The map shows the route that he has taken. How many kilometres has he travelled? His office is at (7,2). Describe how he should travel using the shortest route in kilometres.

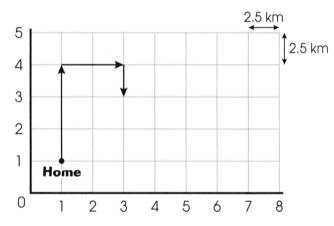

2.5 km

2.5 km

⑬ An adult ticket costs $7 and a child ticket costs $4. A movie theatre made $1092. How many tickets were sold if the number of adult tickets sold was between 95 and 105?

Hints

This question has more than one answer.

Topics covered:

Question 11	**Question 12**	**Question 13**
• fractions	• decimals	• subtraction
• time	• movements	• multiplication
• patterning		

ISBN: 978-1-77149-202-7

⑭ Jessica created a mosaic with tiles that are 2 cm by 3 cm each. She recorded the number of tiles of each colour she used in the bar graph. What is the area of the mosaic?

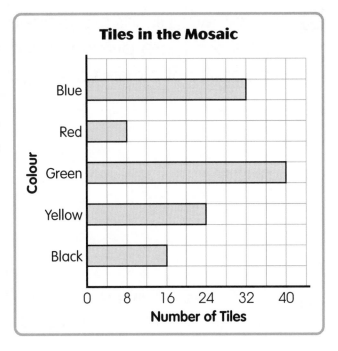

⑮ Refer to Question 14. Jessica added some red tiles and yellow tiles to make the mosaic a square. The perimeter of the mosaic is now 120 cm. What is its area? If the mode number of tiles is now 16, how many yellow tiles were added?

Hints

Find how many new tiles were added using the new area.

Topics covered:

Question 14
- multiplication
- area
- data management

Question 15
- perimeter
- area
- data management

ISBN: 978-1-77149-202-7

The following solids are placed in a bag: 3 cubes, 2 rectangular prisms, 2 square pyramids, 4 cones, and 1 sphere. What is the probability of picking a solid with 8 vertices?

⑰ Four square tables each having a side length of 0.8 m are put together to form a big square. What is the perimeter of the combined square?

⑱ Gordon is making shapes using triangles with 4-cm sides. What is the perimeter of the shape in Frame 7?

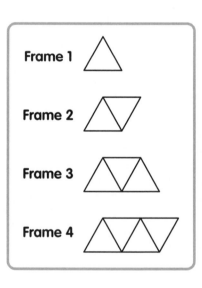

Frame 1

Frame 2

Frame 3

Frame 4

Topics covered:

Question 16	**Question 17**	**Question 18**
• solids	• decimals	• perimeter
• probability	• perimeter	• shapes
	• shapes	• patterning

ISBN: 978-1-77149-202-7

⑲ Kevin will rotate his bed $\frac{1}{4}$ counterclockwise about (5,3). If he wants two corners of his bed to be at (0,2) and (3,0), how should he translate his bed? Describe the translation in metres.

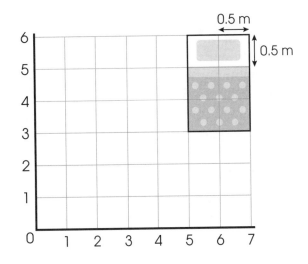

⑳ Anthony wants to make a tiling pattern that measures 92 cm by 68 cm. The pattern is made by triangular prints. How many prints will there be in the pattern?

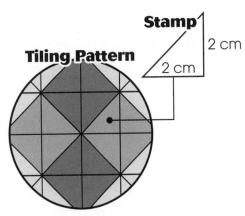

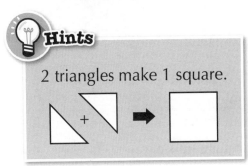

Hints

2 triangles make 1 square.

Topics covered:

Question 19
• decimals
• locations
• movements

Question 20
• multiplication
• division
• area

ISBN: 978-1-77149-202-7

Students are required to solve multi-step questions which involve various topics in each.

Topics Covered

	Number Sense and Numeration	Measurement	Geometry and Spatial Sense	Patterning and Algebra	Data Management and Probability	My Record ✔ correct ✘ incorrect
1	division decimals	perimeter				☐
2	addition subtraction			patterning		☐
3	money				probability	☐
4	multiplication fractions	time				☐
5	division			patterning		☐
6	division fractions					☐
7	money				data management	☐
8		perimeter area	movements			☐
9	subtraction	area				☐
10		time	locations	patterning		☐
11	decimals	perimeter	shapes			☐
12		time		patterning		☐
13		area	shapes locations			☐
14	money			patterning		☐
15		perimeter	shapes			☐
16	addition				probability	☐
17	multiplication fractions					☐
18	multiplication			equations		☐
19			solids		data management	☐
20				patterning	probability	☐

ISBN: 978-1-77149-202-7

① One flower is placed every 10 cm along the border of the garden below. How many flowers are there?

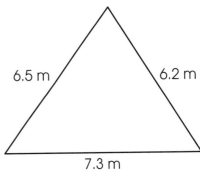

6.5 m   6.2 m

7.3 m

② A ski lodge costs $1760 for the first week and each additional week is $182 cheaper than the previous week. How much does 3 weeks at the ski lodge cost?

③ Omar paid for a $6.70 meal with a $10 bill. He got his change in the fewest coins. He picked a coin randomly to leave as a tip. What is the probability that he picked a loonie?

Topics covered:

Question 1
- division
- decimals
- perimeter

Question 2
- addition
- subtraction
- patterning

Question 3
- money
- probability

ISBN: 978-1-77149-202-7

④ It takes Amina 75 seconds to put icing on a cookie. Will it take her longer than $18\frac{1}{2}$ minutes to put icing on 15 cookies?

⑤ Mr. Matthews is using black and white tiles to create a pattern on a wall. If the wall is 6 m long, how many black tiles does he need?

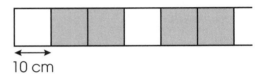

10 cm

⑥ A factory installs 4 wheels on each car and 6 wheels on each bus. There are 1800 wheels and $\frac{2}{3}$ of them are for cars. How many buses will the factory install wheels on?

Topics covered:

Question 4	**Question 5**	**Question 6**
• multiplication	• division	• division
• fractions	• patterning	• fractions
• time		

ISBN: 978-1-77149-202-7

⑦ Melanie counted all the coins in her piggy bank and created a bar graph. Does she have enough money to buy a $10 book?

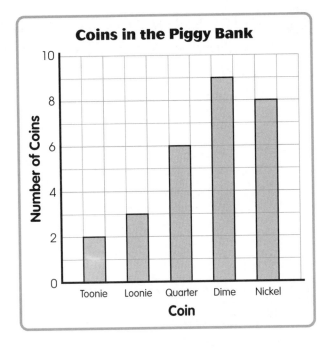

Coins in the Piggy Bank

⑧ A rectangle is cut into 2 equal halves along the dotted line and transformed as shown. Describe the transformation.

If the perimeter of the original rectangle is 8 cm shorter than the transformed shape, what is the area of the original shape?

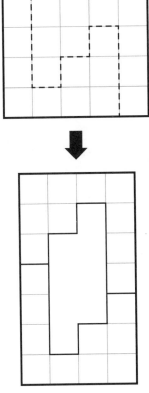

Topics covered:

Question 7
- money
- data management

Question 8
- perimeter
- area
- movements

ISBN: 978-1-77149-202-7

⑨ Tommy's new TV has dimensions of 93 cm and 52 cm. His old TV has dimensions of 71 cm and 40 cm. What is the difference in area?

⑩ A train is located at (10,15). Every 4 minutes, it moves 2 units to the left and 3 units down. When will the train arrive at (0,0) if it leaves at 1:47 p.m.?

⑪ A rectangular desk has a length of 1.5 m and a perimeter of 5 m. Martin puts 2 desks together to form an "L" shape. What is the perimeter of the desks?

Topics covered:

Question 9	Question 10	Question 11
• subtraction	• time	• decimals
• area	• locations	• perimeter
	• patterning	• shapes

ISBN: 978-1-77149-202-7

⑫ The amount of time needed to charge a cell phone is recorded every 6 months. If the pattern continues, would the charging time be less than $\frac{1}{2}$ hour in January 2017?

Time Needed to Charge a Cell Phone

Date	Time
Jan 2014	2 h 15 min
Jul 2014	1 h 55 min
Jan 2015	1 h 35 min
Jul 2015	1 h 15 min

⑬ Shawna wants to draw a rectangle with an area of 108 cm² on the grid. One of its vertices is at (2,2). What are the coordinates of the other vertices? Draw the rectangle.

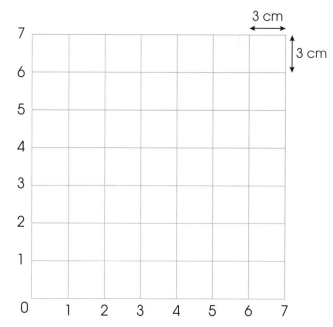

Topics covered:

Question 12
• time
• patterning

Question 13
• area
• shapes
• locations

ISBN: 978-1-77149-202-7

⑭ Ben plans to save $2 in January, $3 in February, $5 in March, and $9 in April. If the pattern continues, will he have enough money to buy a $245.85 game console in August? If so, what will his change be?

⑮ Felicia used 7 skewers of equal lengths to make 2 shapes. The difference in their perimeters is 18 cm. What is the sum of their perimeters?

⑯ 562 boys, 498 girls, 2146 women, and 1794 men participate in a lucky draw. If there is only 1 winner, what is the probability that the winner is an adult?

⑰ There are 36 books in each box. $\frac{1}{10}$ of 100 boxes of books got soaked during shipment. How many books were not soaked?

Topics covered:

Question 14	**Question 15**	**Question 16**	**Question 17**
• money	• perimeter	• addition	• multiplication
• patterning	• shapes	• probability	• fractions

ISBN: 978-1-77149-202-7

⑱ Whitney makes $7 an hour and she works 8 hours a day. How many days does she need to work to afford a $728 computer? Write an equation to find the answer.

⑲ Ian has a collection of 3 triangular prisms, 2 cubes, and 4 hexagonal pyramids. What is the median number of faces in his collection?

⑳ Beatrice makes a net for a dice. The numbers on the net follow a pattern down the column and across the row. Write the missing number. What is the probability that a number greater than 500 will be rolled?

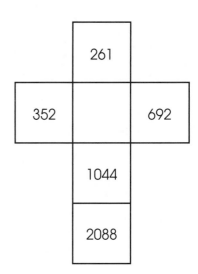

Topics covered:

Question 18	**Question 19**	**Question 20**
• multiplication	• solids	• patterning
• equations	• data management	• probability

ISBN: 978-1-77149-202-7

Students are required to solve multi-step questions which involve various topics in each.

Topics Covered

	Number Sense and Numeration	Measurement	Geometry and Spatial Sense	Patterning and Algebra	Data Management and Probability	My Record ✔ correct ✗ incorrect
1	money				probability	
2		perimeter area	solids			
3	fractions				probability	
4	fractions decimals	time				
5		time		patterning		
6	decimals	time			data management	
7	decimals	perimeter	shapes			
8			solids	equations		
9	fractions	time				
10	subtraction			patterning		
11	multiplication fractions					
12		perimeter area	solids			
13	decimals				probability	
14	multiplication division	time				
15	addition subtraction			patterning		
16		area	shapes movements			
17	division fractions	area				
18	decimals				data management	
19	decimals				data management	
20	subtraction fractions					

ISBN: 978-1-77149-202-7

① Ms. Chan organizes 4 stacks of $200 in which each stack has exactly 6 bills and no 2 stacks are the same. If a bill is picked from a stack, what is the probability that it is a $100 bill?

② Andy has 4 identical triangles, each having 3 equal sides, an area of 11 cm², and a perimeter of 15 cm. He uses them to make the net of a triangular pyramid. Draw the net. What is the perimeter and area of the net?

Topics covered:

Question 1
- money
- probability

Question 2
- perimeter
- area
- solids

ISBN: 978-1-77149-202-7

③ A Grade 4 class has 16 boys and 14 girls. On a test, $\frac{1}{4}$ of the boys and $\frac{1}{2}$ of the girls received an A grade. What is the probability of choosing a student who did not get an A?

④ Laura is doing a 10-km charity run. She has completed 0.8 of the race in $\frac{5}{6}$ hour. If she wants to finish the race in an hour, in how many minutes does she need to run each remaining kilometre?

⑤ The amount of time Joshua spent on trombone practice follows a pattern. Will he spend more than 3 hours practising next week if the pattern continues?

Time Spent on Trombone Practice

Day	No. of Minutes
Mon	15
Tue	20
Wed	17
Thu	22
Fri	19
Sat	24
Sun	21

Topics covered:

Question 3	**Question 4**	**Question 5**
• fractions	• fractions	• time
• probability	• decimals	• patterning
	• time	

ISBN: 978-1-77149-202-7

⑥ Nicole swam 5 laps in 2 min 43 s. Her fastest time was 30.8 s, her median time was 31.6 s, and there was no mode time. What was her longest possible time?

⑦ A race track is composed of 2 rectangles. How far will a race car travel if it goes around the track 3 times?

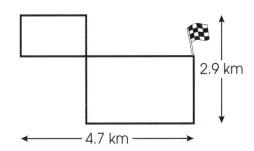

2.9 km

4.7 km

⑧ Write an equation relating the number of faces in a prism and the number of sides in its base. Then name the prism that has 10 faces.

⑨ It takes $2\frac{3}{4}$ hours to upload a video and $1\frac{5}{6}$ hours to upload a document. How long, in hours and minutes, does it take to upload both files?

Topics covered:

Question 6	**Question 7**	**Question 8**	**Question 9**
• decimals	• decimals	• solids	• fractions
• time	• perimeter	• equations	• time
• data management	• shapes		

ISBN: 978-1-77149-202-7

⑩ An organization holds an annual release of salmon into the wild. Each year, they release an additional 1300 salmon than the previous year. How many salmon were released in 2011 if 10 000 salmon were released in 2016?

⑪ In a package of 100 folders, $\frac{1}{5}$ are red, $\frac{3}{10}$ are blue, and the rest are green. How many blue and green folders are there in 55 packages?

⑫ The net of a triangular prism has 2 triangles and 3 squares. It has a perimeter of 180 cm. What is the area of one of the squares?

Topics covered:

Question 10	**Question 11**	**Question 12**
• subtraction	• multiplication	• perimeter
• patterning	• fractions	• area
		• solids

ISBN: 978-1-77149-202-7

⑬ There are 30 students in a class. 0.5 of the students have black hair, 0.2 have blonde hair, and the rest have brown hair. If a student calls in sick, what is the probability that the student has brown hair?

⑭ A barista makes 13 cups of latte every 5 minutes. How many cups of latte can she make in 2 hours?

⑮ A concert venue is divided into 5 sections. Section 1 holds 1002 people, Section 2 holds 2013 people, Section 3 holds 3024 people, and so on. How many people can the concert venue hold in total?

Topics covered:

Question 13	**Question 14**	**Question 15**
• decimals	• multiplication	• addition
• probability	• division	• subtraction
	• time	• patterning

ISBN: 978-1-77149-202-7

Paula created 2 shapes using a triangular stamp. She slid the stamp 3 cm to the left for one shape and for the other shape, she slid the stamp 6 cm down. Name the shapes. Which shape has a greater area?

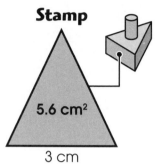

Stamp

5.6 cm²

3 cm

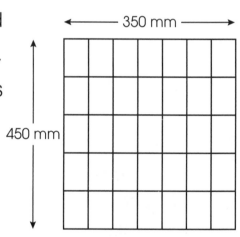 35 black and red cards are arranged as shown. If $\frac{3}{7}$ of the cards are black, what is the area of all the black cards in square centimetres?

350 mm

450 mm

Topics covered:

Question 16
- area
- shapes
- movements

Question 17
- division
- fractions
- area

ISBN: 978-1-77149-202-7

⑱ The bar graph shows the precipitation in 3 cities in one day. How much more precipitation did Ottawa get than Toronto?

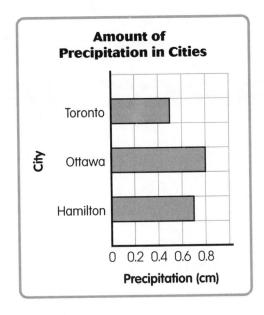

⑲ Refer to Question 18. The precipitation in Sudbury is added to the graph. Its precipitation is the new median and mode of the set of data. How much more precipitation did Sudbury get than Toronto?

⑳ An auditorium is $\frac{2}{5}$ full, with 2020 people. How many more people can the auditorium hold?

Topics covered:

Question 18	**Question 19**	**Question 20**
• decimals	• decimals	• subtraction
• data management	• data management	• fractions

Students are required to solve multi-step questions which involve various topics in each.

Topics Covered

	Number Sense and Numeration	Measurement	Geometry and Spatial Sense	Patterning and Algebra	Data Management and Probability	My Record ✔ correct ✘ incorrect
1	decimals fractions					☐
2	addition subtraction			patterning		☐
3	fractions	perimeter area				☐
4	money	time				☐
5	addition fractions					☐
6	fractions	time		patterning		☐
7		area	movements			☐
8		time	movements			☐
9	addition division	perimeter				☐
10	multiplication division	area				☐
11	decimals			patterning		☐
12		perimeter area	locations movements			☐
13	multiplication fractions				probability	☐
14	money	time			data management	☐
15		perimeter area				☐
16	division		locations movements			☐
17	division decimals					☐
18	subtraction multiplication					☐
19		perimeter			data management	☐
20					probability / data management	☐

ISBN: 978-1-77149-202-7

① Kyle swims 1.3 km. Mark swims $\frac{11}{10}$ km. Who swims farther and by how much?

② Hot dogs were sold during a 3-hour baseball game. Each hour, 346 more hot dogs were sold than the previous hour. If 3224 hot dogs were sold in the third hour, how many hot dogs were sold in total?

③ A 48 cm by 32 cm rectangular pizza is cut into 8 cm by 8 cm square slices. What is the area of each slice? What fraction of the slices do not have any crust?

Topics covered:

Question 1	**Question 2**	**Question 3**
• decimals	• addition	• fractions
• fractions	• subtraction	• perimeter
	• patterning	• area

ISBN: 978-1-77149-202-7

④ Michelle was charged for using the Internet on a cruise ship, which included an activation fee of $2.85 and $0.75 for each minute. How long did Michelle use the Internet for if she was charged $10.35?

⑤ A white string is $\frac{3}{4}$ of the length of a blue string, and a red string is $1\frac{2}{3}$ the length of the white string. What is the total length of the 3 strings if the blue string is 24 cm?

⑥ The sunrise time is recorded on the first day of each week. The sun rises at 6:45 a.m. in Week 1, 6:51 a.m. in Week 2, and 6:57 a.m. in Week 3. In which week will the sun rise $\frac{1}{2}$ hour later than Week 1?

Topics covered:

Question 4	Question 5	Question 6
• money	• addition	• fractions
• time	• fractions	• time
		• patterning

ISBN: 978-1-77149-202-7

⑦ Hilary folds a piece of paper in half along the dotted line and draws half of a shape as shown. She will complete it by drawing a reflection over the dotted line. Draw to complete the shape. What is the area of the shape?

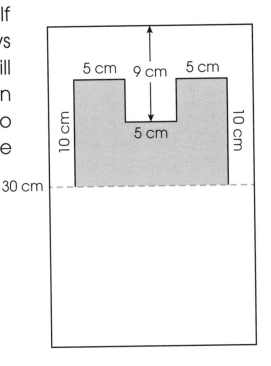

⑧ It takes Stephanie 6 min to walk up and 4 min to walk to the left from her house to the park. How long does it take her to walk from the park to the cafe and then back home?

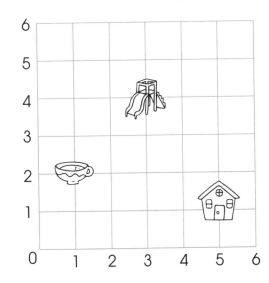

Topics covered:

Question 7
- area
- movements

Question 8
- time
- movements

ISBN: 978-1-77149-202-7

⑨ Field A is 1784 m long and 2412 m wide. Field B's perimeter is half of Field A's and it has a length of 1492 m. What is the width of Field B?

⑩ The cost of lawn mowing is based on the lawn's area. Trevor's front yard measures 12 m by 14 m and the cost is $8. What is the area of his backyard if it costs $10 to mow it?

⑪ A subway token costs $3.40 today. The cost increased by 15 cents in each of the past 5 years. If Larry purchased 8 tokens 5 years ago, how much money did he save?

Topics covered:

Question 9	**Question 10**	**Question 11**
• addition	• multiplication	• decimals
• division	• division	• patterning
• perimeter	• area	

ISBN: 978-1-77149-202-7

⑫ Rana rotates the figure $\frac{1}{4}$ clockwise about (4,4) three times to make a shape. What is the shape? If the perimeter of the shape is 96 cm, what is its area?

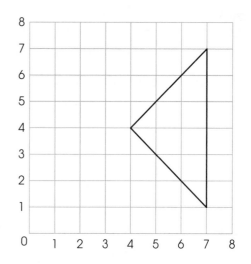

⑬ 2400 balls are in a ball pit. $\frac{1}{4}$ of the balls are red, there are twice as many blue balls as the red balls, and the rest are green balls. If a ball is picked randomly, what is the probability that it is red or green?

⑭ At a charity basketball game, each shot was worth 25 cents. The number of shots made each hour was recorded in the graph. How much was made in donations after 5:00?

Number of Basketball Shots in Each Hour

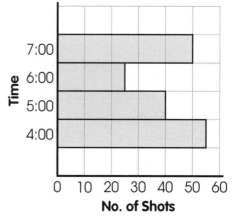

Topics covered:

Question 12	Question 13	Question 14
• perimeter	• multiplication	• money
• area	• fractions	• time
• locations	• probability	• data management
• movements		

ISBN: 978-1-77149-202-7

⑮ A brochure has an area of 621 cm² when unfolded. What is the perimeter of the folded brochure?

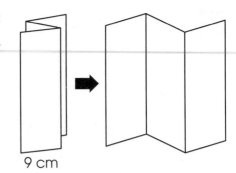

9 cm

⑯ Lucy walked from (6,1) to (3,5) along the grid on a map. What is the distance of each unit of the grid if she walked 1092 cm in total?

⑰ White road markings are added as shown. How many white markings does a 1-km road have?

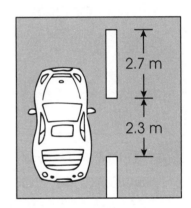

2.7 m

2.3 m

⑱ A store warehouse has 4212 boxes. Each box has 10 toys. If 2011 boxes are shipped out, how many toys are left in the warehouse?

Topics covered:

Question 15	**Question 16**	**Question 17**	**Question 18**
• perimeter	• division	• division	• subtraction
• area	• locations	• decimals	• multiplication
	• movements		

ISBN: 978-1-77149-202-7

19. The floor plan shows 5 rooms. What is the median perimeter of the rooms?

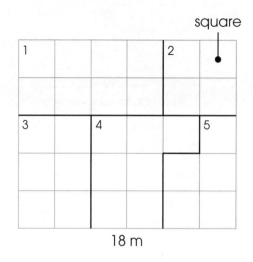

square

18 m

20. The bar graph shows the students' marks. What is the probability of picking a student with a mark higher than the median?

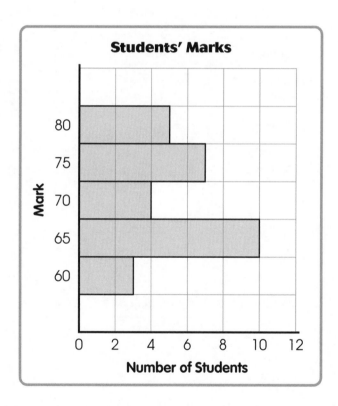

Topics covered:

Question 19
- perimeter
- data management

Question 20
- data management
- probability

ISBN: 978-1-77149-202-7

Students are required to solve multi-step questions which involve various topics in each.

Topics Covered

	Number Sense and Numeration	Measurement	Geometry and Spatial Sense	Patterning and Algebra	Data Management and Probability	My Record ✔ correct ✘ incorrect
1	multiplication			patterning		☐
2	division	area				☐
3	fractions				data management	☐
4	addition				data management	☐
5		perimeter area		equations		☐
6	fractions	time				☐
7	multiplication money		solids			☐
8	decimals				probability	☐
9	subtraction money					☐
10	multiplication		locations movements			☐
11	multiplication				data management	☐
12	fractions money					☐
13	division	perimeter	shapes			☐
14	money			patterning		☐
15	fractions				probability	☐
16	decimals	area				☐
17	multiplication	perimeter	shapes			☐
18			movements	patterning		☐
19		perimeter area	movements			☐
20	division money	area				☐

ISBN: 978-1-77149-202-7

① During a promotion week, 7 shirts are given out on the 1st day, 20 shirts on the 2nd day, and 33 shirts on the 3rd day. Each shirt costs $25. If the pattern continues, what is the total cost of all the shirts given out on the 7th day?

② Alana sells 3 trays of lemon squares for $120. Each lemon square is 3 cm by 3 cm. How much does each lemon square cost?

15 cm

1 tray of lemon squares

6 cm

③ Iris's 8 friends are from 10 to 12 years old. $\frac{1}{4}$ of them are 10 years old and $\frac{1}{2}$ of them are 11 years old. What are the median and mode ages?

Topics covered:

Question 1	**Question 2**	**Question 3**
• multiplication	• division	• fractions
• patterning	• area	• data management

ISBN: 978-1-77149-202-7

④ The bar graph shows the number of visitors to the museum. How many visitors were there from June to August?

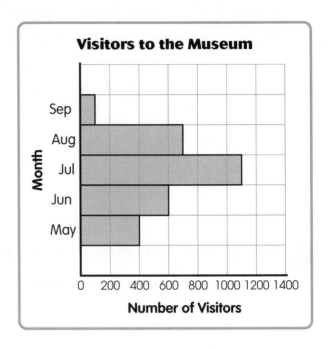

Visitors to the Museum

⑤ The perimeter of a rectangle is 100 cm. The length is 30 cm. Write an equation to find the width. What is the area of the rectangle?

Topics covered:

Question 4
- addition
- data management

Question 5
- perimeter
- area
- equations

ISBN: 978-1-77149-202-7

⑥ In June, Travis spent $\frac{1}{5}$ of the days at his cottage, $\frac{2}{3}$ on a trip, and the rest at home. How many days did he spend at home?

⑦ 160 rectangular prisms and 212 square-based pyramids are made with sticks and balls of modelling clay. One pack of modelling clay costs $35.50 and can make 1000 balls. How much does the modelling clay for all the solids cost?

⑧ Raymond has 200 sheets of notes. 0.5 of them are on Science, 0.1 are on French, and the rest are on Math. His cat tore 1 of the sheets. What is the probability that it was a sheet of Math notes?

⑨ Jerry had 1020 dimes. He spent 409 dimes and traded the remaining dimes for the fewest bills and coins. How many $20 bills did he get?

Topics covered:

Question 6	**Question 7**	**Question 8**	**Question 9**
• fractions	• multiplication	• decimals	• subtraction
• time	• money	• probability	• money
	• solids		

ISBN: 978-1-77149-202-7

⑩ A bird flew along the grid from (1,1) to (5,1) to (5,5) to (2,5). What is the total distance that the bird flew?

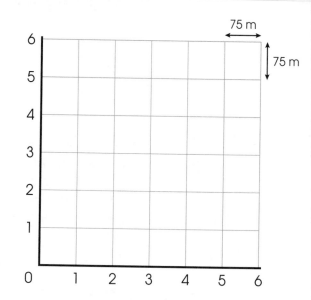

⑪ Taylor created a bar graph on the books that she sold at her store. She made $396 from the books but she forgot how many books that cost $9 were sold. Help her solve the problem and complete the bar graph.

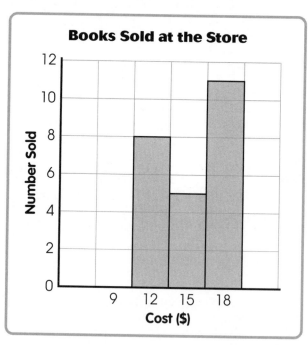

Topics covered:

Question 10
- multiplication
- locations
- movements

Question 11
- multiplication
- data management

ISBN: 978-1-77149-202-7

⑫ Lily spent $14.95 on a baseball ticket and $5 on snacks. She has $5.05 left. What fraction of her money did she spend on snacks?

⑬ Nicky walks his dog around a kite-shaped field. Nicky walks 2 m every second while his dog walks 3 m. How many more seconds does it take Nicky to walk around the field than his dog?

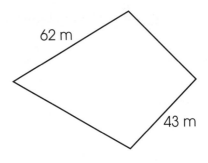

62 m

43 m

⑭ Isabel spends $23.54 on Monday, $38.78 on Tuesday, $54.02 on Wednesday, and so on. If she starts with $1000, how much will she have left after Thursday?

Topics covered:

Question 12	**Question 13**	**Question 14**
• fractions	• division	• money
• money	• perimeter	• patterning
	• shapes	

⑮ Joey has a stamp collection. $\frac{1}{4}$ of the stamps are from North America, $\frac{1}{3}$ from Europe, $\frac{1}{6}$ from Africa, and the rest are from Asia. Joey has 30 stamps from North America. If one stamp is picked randomly, what is the probability that it is from Asia?

⑯ Ms. Ma's classroom is 30 m long and 20 m wide. Mr. Hamilton's classroom has dimensions that are 0.8 of Ms. Ma's. What is the area of Mr. Hamilton's classroom?

⑰ There are 15 squares and 12 triangles each with a side length of 15 cm. What is the total perimeter of the shapes?

Topics covered:

Question 15	Question 16	Question 17
• fractions	• decimals	• multiplication
• probability	• area	• perimeter
		• shapes

ISBN: 978-1-77149-202-7

⑱ Ted has 2 types of tiles. He transformed the L as shown. Follow the same pattern and transform the ⊏. Describe the pattern.

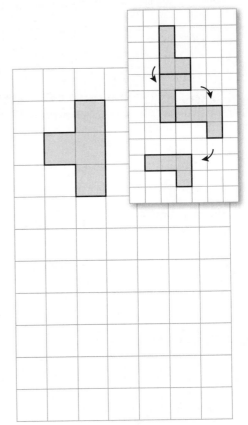

⑲ Refer to Question 18. Ted combines 4 ⊏ to make a square. Draw to show how they are combined. The perimeter of ⊏ is 20 cm. What is the area of the square?

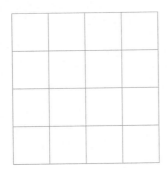

⑳ Refer to Question 19. Each tile costs 8¢. How much money is needed to tile a 40 cm by 40 cm area?

Topics covered:

Question 18
- movements
- patterning

Question 19
- perimeter
- area
- movements

Question 20
- division
- money
- area

ISBN: 978-1-77149-202-7

10

Students are required to solve multi-step questions which involve various topics in each.

Topics Covered

	Number Sense and Numeration	Measurement	Geometry and Spatial Sense	Patterning and Algebra	Data Management and Probability	My Record ✔ correct ✘ incorrect
1	division money	perimeter				☐
2	subtraction fractions					☐
3	addition				probability	☐
4	multiplication	time				☐
5	multiplication				data management	☐
6	division				data management	☐
7		perimeter		patterning		☐
8	division		solids			☐
9	multiplication	time				☐
10				equations	probability	☐
11	multiplication	time				☐
12	multiplication		movements	patterning		☐
13	money				probability	☐
14	multiplication	perimeter	shapes			☐
15	decimals	time				☐
16		time			data management	☐
17	decimals			patterning		☐
18		perimeter	shapes solids			☐
19			locations		probability	☐
20		perimeter area			probability	☐

ISBN: 978-1-77149-202-7

① A tree is planted every 3 m around a park. It takes 30 min to plant a tree. If the labour cost is $562.25 for every 10 hours, how much will it cost to plant all the trees?

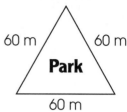

60 m 60 m

Park

60 m

② Team A and Team B both hit 1000 baseballs. $\frac{2}{5}$ of the hits were home runs for Team A and $\frac{1}{4}$ for Team B. Which team hit more home runs and by how many more?

③ There are 1354 trout, 2646 salmon, and 3000 bass in a lake. If a fisherman goes fishing, what is the probability that he will catch a trout or a salmon?

④ It takes Hannah 24 minutes to ride the bus from home to school. If she takes the bus to and from school every day, how many hours does she spend on the bus each week?

Topics covered:

Question 1	**Question 2**	**Question 3**	**Question 4**
• division	• subtraction	• addition	• multiplication
• money	• fractions	• probability	• time
• perimeter			

ISBN: 978-1-77149-202-7

⑤ The bar graph shows the number of laps each child swam. Each lap was 100 m. What is the difference between the distances swum by Marc and Ivy?

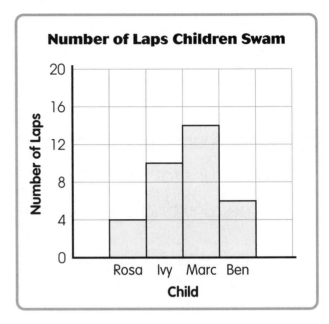

Number of Laps Children Swam

⑥ Refer to Question 5. Rosa swam more laps to catch up so the median distance swum is now 1 km. How many more laps did Rosa swim?

Topics covered:

Question 5
- multiplication
- data management

Question 6
- division
- data management

ISBN: 978-1-77149-202-7

⑦ A sheet of paper is 50 cm long and 20 cm wide. It is cut into 5-cm strips as shown. What is the pattern rule for the perimeter of the piece of paper after each strip is cut? What is its perimeter after 7 strips are cut?

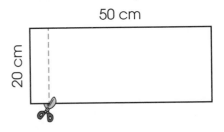

⑧ The sum of the area of all the faces of a cube is 5400 cm². What is the area and side length of each face of the cube?

⑨ Every day, a florist gives out a bouquet of 3 red flowers, 6 white flowers, and 7 yellow flowers. How many more yellow flowers than red flowers does she give out in a leap year?

Topics covered:

Question 7	**Question 8**	**Question 9**
• perimeter	• division	• multiplication
• patterning	• solids	• time

ISBN: 978-1-77149-202-7

⑩ Francis has a stack of yellow, blue, and red cards. The probability of picking a yellow card is 1 out of 5, and there are 12 more blue cards than red cards. If there are 50 cards, how many cards of each colour are there? Write an equation to solve the problem.

⑪ It takes Pamela 12 minutes to make a bracelet and 10 minutes to make a necklace. When will she finish making 11 sets of bracelets and necklaces if she starts at 9:24 a.m.?

⑫ Mike learns a new dance move. For each move, he steps to the left twice and then steps to the right once. If each of his steps is 25 cm, how far from his original position will he be after he does 16 dance moves?

Topics covered:

Question 10	Question 11	Question 12
• equations	• multiplication	• multiplication
• probability	• time	• movements
		• patterning

ISBN: 978-1-77149-202-7

⑬ Ryan and Taylor have some toy bills for a game. Their bills are shown below. If their bills are mixed together and one bill is picked randomly, what is the probability that the bill belongs to the person who has more money?

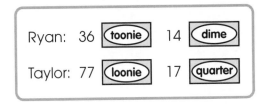

Ryan: 36 (toonie) 14 (dime)

Taylor: 77 (loonie) 17 (quarter)

⑭ James drew a shape that had a side length of 45 cm and 4 lines of symmetry. What shape did he draw? What was its perimeter?

⑮ Connor spends 8.4 hours sleeping, 6.5 hours at school, and 2.6 hours doing extracurricular activities. How many minutes are left in his day?

Topics covered:

Question 13
- money
- probability

Question 14
- multiplication
- perimeter
- shapes

Question 15
- decimals
- time

ISBN: 978-1-77149-202-7

⑯ Charmaine spent 3 hours running 4 errands. The median time was 31 minutes and the mode time was 18 minutes. How much time did each errand take?

⑰ A baby weighed 3.5 kg in Week 1, 3.7 kg in Week 2, and 3.9 kg in Week 3. What was the baby's weight in Week 8?

⑱ Keith uses 1 pentagon and 5 identical triangles to make a pentagonal pyramid. The side lengths of each triangle are equal and the sum of their perimeters is 180 cm. What is the perimeter of the pentagon?

Topics covered:

Question 16	**Question 17**	**Question 18**
• time	• decimals	• perimeter
• data management	• patterning	• shapes
		• solids

ISBN: 978-1-77149-202-7

Laurel hid a treasure on the grid. If a location is randomly picked on the grid, what is the probability of finding the treasure?

Laurel gave the following clues about its location.

- The x-coordinate is smaller than the y-coordinate.
- The sum of the coordinates is 7.

What are the possible locations of the treasure?

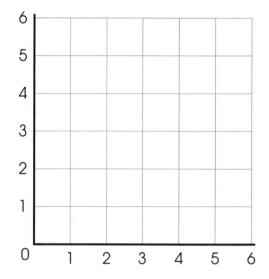

 Mariah puts 5 shapes together to make a house design. The small square has a perimeter of 8 cm and the triangle has an area of 12 cm². If one of the shapes is missing, is it more likely that it has a perimeter greater than 16 cm or an area less than 12 cm²?

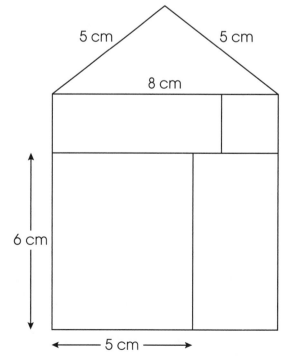

Topics covered:

Question 19
- locations
- probability

Question 20
- perimeter
- area
- probability

ISBN: 978-1-77149-202-7

ISBN: 978-1-77149-202-7

■ Answers

Basic Problem-solving Questions

1 Addition

Math Skills

1. 3515	2. 5355	3. 3596
4. 7706	5. 5772	6. 8482
7. 8959	8. 8936	9. 3207
10. 9433	11. 6524	12. 9280
13. 7839	14. 8068	15. 6965
16. 9213	17. 6937	18. 8445
19. 8596		
20a. 2461	b. 5192	c. 11 497

Problem Solving

5258 ; 5258 ; 5258

1. 1733 + 3652 = 5385
   5385
   $$\begin{array}{r} 1733 \\ + 3652 \\ \hline 5385 \end{array}$$

2. $3805 + $2987 = $6792
   6792
   $$\begin{array}{r} 3805 \\ + 2987 \\ \hline 6792 \end{array}$$

3a. 2456 + 1647 = 4103
    4103
    $$\begin{array}{r} 2456 \\ + 1647 \\ \hline 4103 \end{array}$$

b. 2456 + 4103 = 6559
   6559
   $$\begin{array}{r} 2456 \\ + 4103 \\ \hline 6559 \end{array}$$

4a. 1912 + 1048 = 2960
    2960
    $$\begin{array}{r} 1912 \\ + 1048 \\ \hline 2960 \end{array}$$

b. 2960 + 2960 = 5920
   5920
   $$\begin{array}{r} 2960 \\ + 2960 \\ \hline 5920 \end{array}$$

5. 2750 + 2750 + 2750 = 8250
   8250
   $$\begin{array}{r} 2750 \\ 2750 \\ + 2750 \\ \hline 8250 \end{array}$$

6. 4096 + 4096 + 496 = 8688
   There were 8688 people
   at the game.
   $$\begin{array}{r} 4096 \\ 4096 \\ + 496 \\ \hline 8688 \end{array}$$

7a. 2870 + 2593 = 5463
    Rosanna biked 5463 m
    on the weekend.
    $$\begin{array}{r} 2870 \\ + 2593 \\ \hline 5463 \end{array}$$

b. 1710 + 3417 + 3229 = 8356
   Rosanna biked 8356 m
   on the weekdays.
   $$\begin{array}{r} 1710 \\ 3417 \\ + 3229 \\ \hline 8356 \end{array}$$

c. 5463 + 8356 = 13 819
   Rosanna biked 13 819 m
   last week.
   $$\begin{array}{r} 5463 \\ + 8356 \\ \hline 13819 \end{array}$$

8a. Abby: 3469 + 2964 + 5691
    = 12 124
    Abby had a total score of 12 124.
    $$\begin{array}{r} 3469 \\ 2964 \\ + 5691 \\ \hline 12124 \end{array}$$

Ben: 4203 + 3703 + 3780
= 11 686
Ben had a total score of 11 686.
$$\begin{array}{r} 4203 \\ 3703 \\ + 3780 \\ \hline 11686 \end{array}$$

Cory: 3761 + 1694 + 6245
= 11 700
Cory had a total score of 11 700.
$$\begin{array}{r} 3761 \\ 1694 \\ + 6245 \\ \hline 11700 \end{array}$$

b. Abby: 12 124 + 2419 = 14 543
   Ben: 11 686 + 2507 = 14 193
   Cory: 11 700 + 2468 = 14 168

$$\begin{array}{r} 12124 \\ + 2419 \\ \hline 14543 \end{array} \qquad \begin{array}{r} 11686 \\ + 2507 \\ \hline 14193 \end{array} \qquad \begin{array}{r} 11700 \\ + 2468 \\ \hline 14168 \end{array}$$

Abby had the highest total score and won
the game.

9. 410 + 1231 = 1641
   The weight is 1641 kg.
   $$\begin{array}{r} 410 \\ + 1231 \\ \hline 1641 \end{array}$$

10. 1805 + 3621 = 5426
    The weight is 5426 kg.
    $$\begin{array}{r} 1805 \\ + 3621 \\ \hline 5426 \end{array}$$

11. 4647 + 5209 = 9856
    Martin has 9856 mL
    of purple paint.
    $$\begin{array}{r} 4647 \\ + 5209 \\ \hline 9856 \end{array}$$

12. 330 + 1123 = 1453
    The Byzantine Empire
    ended in the year 1453.
    $$\begin{array}{r} 330 \\ + 1123 \\ \hline 1453 \end{array}$$

13. 2631 + 2069 = 4700
    The recommended daily
    potassium intake is 4700 mg.
    $$\begin{array}{r} 2631 \\ + 2069 \\ \hline 4700 \end{array}$$

14. 1225 + 4798 = 6023
    The speed of the aircraft
    is 6023 km/h.
    $$\begin{array}{r} 1225 \\ + 4798 \\ \hline 6023 \end{array}$$

15. 11 210 + 3583 = 14 793
    The Iliad has 14 793 lines.
    $$\begin{array}{r} 11210 \\ + 3583 \\ \hline 14793 \end{array}$$

16. 2462 + 2462 + 968 = 5892
    Jasmine ran 5892 m in total.
    $$\begin{array}{r} 2462 \\ 2462 \\ + 968 \\ \hline 5892 \end{array}$$

17. 2318 + 2117 + 2117 = 6552
    Mitchell consumed
    6552 calories in total.
    $$\begin{array}{r} 2318 \\ 2117 \\ + 2117 \\ \hline 6552 \end{array}$$

18. Vancouver: 419 + 1038 = 1457
    St. John's: 1457 + 77 = 1534
    The annual average
    precipitation in St. John's
    is 1534 mm.
    $$\begin{array}{r} 419 \\ + 1038 \\ \hline 1457 \\ + 77 \\ \hline 1534 \end{array}$$

2 Subtraction

Math Skills

1. 5768	2. 938	3. 3524
4. 2611	5. 786	6. 3767
7. 936	8. 1413	9. 3828
10. 740	11. 2078	12. 3166
13. 371	14. 4756	15. 2183
16. 2389	17. 5269	18. 3655
19. 4781		

ISBN: 978-1-77149-202-7

20a. 2007   b. 1884

c. 897   d. 1511

Problem Solving

445 ; 445 ; 445

1. 3669 − 2408 = 1261
   1261

$$\begin{array}{r} 3669 \\ -\ 2408 \\ \hline 1261 \end{array}$$

2. 3640 − 1450 = 2190
   2190

$$\begin{array}{r} 3640 \\ -\ 1450 \\ \hline 2190 \end{array}$$

3. 6000 − 3617 = 2383
   2383

$$\begin{array}{r} 6000 \\ -\ 3617 \\ \hline 2383 \end{array}$$

4. $4749 − $1548 = $3201
   3201

$$\begin{array}{r} 4749 \\ -\ 1548 \\ \hline 3201 \end{array}$$

5. 4524 − 3944 = 580
   580

$$\begin{array}{r} 4524 \\ -\ 3944 \\ \hline 580 \end{array}$$

6a. 7551 − 6949 = 602
   602

$$\begin{array}{r} 7551 \\ -\ 6949 \\ \hline 602 \end{array}$$

b. 8600 − 7551 = 1049
   1049

$$\begin{array}{r} 8600 \\ -\ 7551 \\ \hline 1049 \end{array}$$

7a. 1759 − 1397 = 362
   The plant had grown
   362 mm.

$$\begin{array}{r} 1759 \\ -\ 1397 \\ \hline 362 \end{array}$$

b. Year 1 to Year 2: 362
   Year 2 to Year 3: 2089 − 1759 = 330
   Year 3 to Year 4: 2801 − 2089 = 712

$$\begin{array}{r} 2089 \\ -\ 1759 \\ \hline 330 \end{array} \qquad \begin{array}{r} 2801 \\ -\ 2089 \\ \hline 712 \end{array}$$

The plant grew the most between Year 3 and Year 4.

8a. 10 000 − 3075 = 6925
   Dwayne needs to run
   6925 m more.

$$\begin{array}{r} 10000 \\ -\ 3075 \\ \hline 6925 \end{array}$$

b. 4583 − 3684 = 899
   Dwayne ran 899 m
   more in the first 30 minutes.

$$\begin{array}{r} 4583 \\ -\ 3684 \\ \hline 899 \end{array}$$

9. 3706 − 866 − 789 = 2051
   Bernice's current
   elevation is 2051 m.

$$\begin{array}{r} 3706 \\ -\ 866 \\ \hline 2840 \\ -\ 789 \\ \hline 2051 \end{array}$$

10a. $5495 − $2178 = $3317
   The fridge is $3317 now.

$$\begin{array}{r} 5495 \\ -\ 2178 \\ \hline 3317 \end{array}$$

b. $4162 − $3086 = $1076
   The stove is $1076
   cheaper than before.

$$\begin{array}{r} 4162 \\ -\ 3086 \\ \hline 1076 \end{array}$$

c. $3317 − $3086 = $231
   The difference between
   the sale prices of the
   fridge and the stove is $231.

$$\begin{array}{r} 3317 \\ -\ 3086 \\ \hline 231 \end{array}$$

11. 2672 − 1568 = 1104
   The party-sized bag
   has 1104 more calories.

$$\begin{array}{r} 2672 \\ -\ 1568 \\ \hline 1104 \end{array}$$

12. 5769 − 3280 = 2489
   The file size was reduced
   by 2489 MB.

$$\begin{array}{r} 5769 \\ -\ 3280 \\ \hline 2489 \end{array}$$

13. 7821 − 2714 = 5107
   Kelly did not drive along
   5107 km of the Trans-Canada
   Highway.

$$\begin{array}{r} 7821 \\ -\ 2714 \\ \hline 5107 \end{array}$$

14. 11 737 − 6201 = 5536
   A Canadian household
   uses 5536 kWh more electricity.

$$\begin{array}{r} 11737 \\ -\ 6201 \\ \hline 5536 \end{array}$$

15. 10 511 − 7948 = 2563
   2563 more solar panels
   were sold.

$$\begin{array}{r} 10511 \\ -\ 7948 \\ \hline 2563 \end{array}$$

16. 10 000 − 8253 = 1747
   Michelle can add 1747 g
   to her bag at most.

$$\begin{array}{r} 10000 \\ -\ 8253 \\ \hline 1747 \end{array}$$

17. 12 184 − 4600 = 7584
   The airplane must decrease
   its altitude by at least 7584 m.

$$\begin{array}{r} 12184 \\ -\ 4600 \\ \hline 7584 \end{array}$$

18. 6291 − 2670 − 1614 = 2007
   2007 forest fires do not
   have a known cause.

$$\begin{array}{r} 6291 \\ -\ 2670 \\ \hline 3621 \\ -\ 1614 \\ \hline 2007 \end{array}$$

19. Indian Ocean: 10 911 − 2864 = 8047
   Atlantic Ocean: 8047 − 4708 = 3339

$$\begin{array}{r} 10911 \\ -\ 2864 \\ \hline 8047 \end{array} \qquad \begin{array}{r} 8047 \\ -\ 4708 \\ \hline 3339 \end{array}$$

The average depth of the Altantic Ocean is 3339 m.

20. Couch: $4289 − $3618 = $671
   Table: $3206 − $2889 = $317
   Difference: $671 − $317 = $354

$$\begin{array}{r} 4289 \\ -\ 3618 \\ \hline 671 \end{array} \qquad \begin{array}{r} 3206 \\ -\ 2889 \\ \hline 317 \end{array} \qquad \begin{array}{r} 671 \\ -\ 317 \\ \hline 354 \end{array}$$

$354 more is saved on the couch than on the table.

3 Multiplication

Math Skills

1. 297   2. 335

3. 324   4. 1350

5.
$$\begin{array}{r} 56 \\ \times\ 12 \\ \hline 112 \\ 560 \\ \hline 672 \end{array}$$

6.
$$\begin{array}{r} 13 \\ \times\ 49 \\ \hline 117 \\ 520 \\ \hline 637 \end{array}$$

7.
$$\begin{array}{r} 31 \\ \times\ 86 \\ \hline 186 \\ 2480 \\ \hline 2666 \end{array}$$

8.
$$\begin{array}{r} 52 \\ \times\ 63 \\ \hline 156 \\ 3120 \\ \hline 3276 \end{array}$$

ISBN: 978-1-77149-202-7

9. 536   10. 146   11. 498
12. 1352   13. 1210   14. 4697
15. 1012   16. 1053   17. 3060
18. 924   19. 731   20. 6076
21a. 18 ; 25 ; 450   b. 18 ; 100 ; 1800
22a. 24 ; 36 ; 864   b. 24 ; 60 ; 1440

Problem Solving

832 ; 832 ; 832

1. $128 \times 6 = 768$
768

$$\begin{array}{r} 128 \\ \times\ 6 \\ \hline 768 \end{array}$$

2. $200 \times 8 = 1600$
1600

$$\begin{array}{r} 200 \\ \times\ 8 \\ \hline 1600 \end{array}$$

3. $596 \times 3 = 1788$
1788

$$\begin{array}{r} 596 \\ \times\ 3 \\ \hline 1788 \end{array}$$

4. $\$2 \times 216 = \$432$
432

$$\begin{array}{r} 216 \\ \times\ 2 \\ \hline 432 \end{array}$$

5. $12 \times 12 = 144$
144

$$\begin{array}{r} 12 \\ \times\ 12 \\ \hline 24 \\ 120 \\ \hline 144 \end{array}$$

6a. $34 \times 26 = 884$
884

$$\begin{array}{r} 34 \\ \times\ 26 \\ \hline 204 \\ 680 \\ \hline 884 \end{array}$$

b. $\$8 \times 884 = \$7072$
7072

$$\begin{array}{r} 884 \\ \times\ 8 \\ \hline 7072 \end{array}$$

7a. $27 \times 11 = 297$
297 robots are built.

$$\begin{array}{r} 27 \\ \times\ 11 \\ \hline 27 \\ 270 \\ \hline 297 \end{array}$$

b. $297 \times 100 = 29\ 700$
29 700 mL of paint is needed.

8. $45 \times 31 = 1395$
Michael will eat 1395 raisins
in January.

$$\begin{array}{r} 45 \\ \times\ 31 \\ \hline 45 \\ 1350 \\ \hline 1395 \end{array}$$

9. $10 \times 365 = 3650$
No, Olivia will not finish the series in a
year.

10. Package 1: $36 \times 4 \times 10 = 1440$
Package 2: $195 \times 2 \times 4 = 1560$
Package 3: $54 \times 10 \times 3 = 1620$
Jasper should buy Package 3 to get the
most chocolate.

11a. 2 weeks = 14 days
$15 \times 14 = 210$
Lawrence folds
210 paper stars in 2 weeks.

$$\begin{array}{r} 15 \\ \times\ 14 \\ \hline 60 \\ 150 \\ \hline 210 \end{array}$$

b. $210 \times 9 = 1890$
18 m = 1800 cm
No, a roll of 18-m paper
is not enough.

$$\begin{array}{r} 210 \\ \times\ 9 \\ \hline 1890 \end{array}$$

12a. $16 \times 53 = 848$
There are 848 students
at the swim meet.

$$\begin{array}{r} 16 \\ \times\ 53 \\ \hline 48 \\ 800 \\ \hline 848 \end{array}$$

b. $12 \times 70 = 840$
No, not all the students are
scheduled to race.

$$\begin{array}{r} 12 \\ \times\ 70 \\ \hline 840 \end{array}$$

c. $\$5 \times 848 = \$4240$
$4240 is collected in total.

$$\begin{array}{r} 848 \\ \times\ 5 \\ \hline 4240 \end{array}$$

13a. $76 \times 16 = 1216$
No, 16 people cannot
ride the elevator.

$$\begin{array}{r} 76 \\ \times\ 16 \\ \hline 456 \\ 760 \\ \hline 1216 \end{array}$$

b. $1164 \times 5 = 5820$
The elevator can carry
5820 kg in 5 trips.

$$\begin{array}{r} 1164 \\ \times\ 5 \\ \hline 5820 \end{array}$$

14a. $66 \times 64 = 4224$
The maximum number
of passengers is 4224.

$$\begin{array}{r} 66 \\ \times\ 64 \\ \hline 264 \\ 3960 \\ \hline 4224 \end{array}$$

b. $108 \times 40 = 4320$
The maximum number
of passengers will increase.

$$\begin{array}{r} 108 \\ \times\ 40 \\ \hline 4320 \end{array}$$

15. $76 \times 13 = 988$
No, the truck cannot travel
1000 km in 13 hours.

$$\begin{array}{r} 76 \\ \times\ 13 \\ \hline 228 \\ 760 \\ \hline 988 \end{array}$$

16. Royal Concert Hall: $56 \times 28 = 1568$
Alexander Music Hall: $45 \times 34 = 1530$

$$\begin{array}{r} 56 \\ \times\ 28 \\ \hline 448 \\ 1120 \\ \hline 1568 \end{array} \qquad \begin{array}{r} 45 \\ \times\ 34 \\ \hline 180 \\ 1350 \\ \hline 1530 \end{array}$$

Royal Concert Hall has a higher capacity.

17. $\$75 \times 3 \times 6 = \$1350$
$1350 will be awarded
after 6 nights.

$$\begin{array}{r} 75 \\ \times\ 3 \\ \hline 225 \end{array} \qquad \begin{array}{r} 225 \\ \times\ 6 \\ \hline 1350 \end{array}$$

4 Division

Math Skills

1. $$\begin{array}{r} 50 \\ 6\overline{)300} \\ \underline{300} \end{array}$$

2. $$\begin{array}{r} 91 \\ 9\overline{)819} \\ \underline{81} \\ 9 \\ \underline{9} \end{array}$$

ISBN: 978-1-77149-202-7

3.
$$\begin{array}{r} 67 \\ 4\overline{)268} \\ \underline{24} \\ 28 \\ \underline{28} \end{array}$$

4.
$$\begin{array}{r} 91R2 \\ 5\overline{)457} \\ \underline{45} \\ 7 \\ \underline{5} \\ 2 \end{array}$$

5.
$$\begin{array}{r} 132R4 \\ 6\overline{)796} \\ \underline{6} \\ 19 \\ \underline{18} \\ 16 \\ \underline{12} \\ 4 \end{array}$$

6.
$$\begin{array}{r} 229 \\ 3\overline{)687} \\ \underline{6} \\ 8 \\ \underline{6} \\ 27 \\ \underline{27} \end{array}$$

7.
$$\begin{array}{r} 1204 \\ 2\overline{)2408} \\ \underline{2} \\ 4 \\ \underline{4} \\ 8 \\ \underline{8} \end{array}$$

8.
$$\begin{array}{r} 1037 \\ 4\overline{)4148} \\ \underline{4} \\ 14 \\ \underline{12} \\ 28 \\ \underline{28} \end{array}$$

9. 98R1
10. 81R3
11. 93
12. 192
13. 31R1
14. 107R7
15. 22R3
16. 89R2
17. 249R4
18. 288R2
19. 149R6
20. 1005
21. 367R5
22a. $504 \div 7$; 72   b. $504 \div 8$; 63 (oranges)

Problem Solving

14 ;
$$\begin{array}{r} 14 \\ 8\overline{)112} \\ \underline{8} \\ 32 \\ \underline{32} \end{array}$$
; 14

1. $133 \div 7 = 19$
$$\begin{array}{r} 19 \\ 7\overline{)133} \\ \underline{7} \\ 63 \\ \underline{63} \end{array}$$
19

2. $231 \div 7 = 33$
$$\begin{array}{r} 33 \\ 7\overline{)231} \\ \underline{21} \\ 21 \\ \underline{21} \end{array}$$
33

3a. $8000 \div 10 = 800$
800

b. $800 \div 100 = 8$
8

4. $175 \div 6 = 29R1$
$$\begin{array}{r} 29R1 \\ 6\overline{)175} \\ \underline{12} \\ 55 \\ \underline{54} \\ 1 \end{array}$$
29

5. $237 \div 5 = 47R2$
$$\begin{array}{r} 47R2 \\ 5\overline{)237} \\ \underline{20} \\ 37 \\ \underline{35} \\ 2 \end{array}$$
48

6. $7640 \div 8 = 955$
$$\begin{array}{r} 955 \\ 8\overline{)7640} \\ \underline{72} \\ 44 \\ \underline{40} \\ 40 \\ \underline{40} \end{array}$$
955

7. $4515 \div 9 = 501R6$
$$\begin{array}{r} 501R6 \\ 9\overline{)4515} \\ \underline{45} \\ 15 \\ \underline{9} \\ 6 \end{array}$$
501 cm of ribbon can be used for each gift.

8. $500 \div 3 = 166R2$
Each person got $166 and $2 went to charity.
$$\begin{array}{r} 166R2 \\ 3\overline{)500} \\ \underline{3} \\ 20 \\ \underline{18} \\ 20 \\ \underline{18} \\ 2 \end{array}$$

9a. $1470 \div 7 = 210$
On average, $210 was made in one day.
$$\begin{array}{r} 210 \\ 7\overline{)1470} \\ \underline{14} \\ 70 \\ \underline{70} \end{array}$$

b. Cookies sold:
$210 \div 5 = 42$
Bags of cookies sold:
$42 \div 6 = 7$
On average, 7 bags of cookies were sold each day.
$$\begin{array}{r} 42 \\ 5\overline{)210} \\ \underline{20} \\ 10 \\ \underline{10} \end{array}$$

10a. $1743 \div 3 = 581$
There are 581 toy blocks.
$$\begin{array}{r} 581 \\ 3\overline{)1743} \\ \underline{15} \\ 24 \\ \underline{24} \\ 3 \\ \underline{3} \end{array}$$

b. $581 \div 8 = 72R5$
The remaining 5 toy blocks are not enough for another big block. Thomas can make 72 big blocks.
$$\begin{array}{r} 72R5 \\ 8\overline{)581} \\ \underline{56} \\ 21 \\ \underline{16} \\ 5 \end{array}$$

11. $163 \div 5 = 32R3$
$32 is not enough to pay for dinner. Each person paid at least $33.
$$\begin{array}{r} 32R3 \\ 5\overline{)163} \\ \underline{15} \\ 13 \\ \underline{10} \\ 3 \end{array}$$

12. $5426 \div 4 = 1356R2$
The remaining 2 cobs of corn will each go into a truck. 2 trucks will have 1357 cobs of corn and the other 2 trucks will have 1356 cobs of corn.
$$\begin{array}{r} 1356R2 \\ 4\overline{)5426} \\ \underline{4} \\ 14 \\ \underline{12} \\ 22 \\ \underline{20} \\ 26 \\ \underline{24} \\ 2 \end{array}$$

13a. $627 \div 4 = 156R3$
The remaining 3 beets need 1 more beet to make a pack of 4. 1 more beet is needed so that there are no leftovers.
$$\begin{array}{r} 156R3 \\ 4\overline{)627} \\ \underline{4} \\ 22 \\ \underline{20} \\ 27 \\ \underline{24} \\ 3 \end{array}$$

b. $627 \div 8 = 78R3$
The remaining 3 beets need 5 more beets to make a pack of 8. 5 more beets are needed so that there are no leftovers.
$$\begin{array}{r} 78R3 \\ 8\overline{)627} \\ \underline{56} \\ 67 \\ \underline{64} \\ 3 \end{array}$$

ISBN: 978-1-77149-202-7

14a. $3640 \div 6 = 606R4$

The remaining \$4 is not enough for another slice. The students can afford 606 slices of pizza.

$$\begin{array}{r} 606R4 \\ 6\overline{)3640} \\ \underline{36} \\ 40 \\ \underline{36} \\ 4 \end{array}$$

b. $606 \div 8 = 75R6$

The remaining 6 slices do not make one pizza. The students can order 75 pizzas.

$$\begin{array}{r} 75R6 \\ 8\overline{)606} \\ \underline{56} \\ 46 \\ \underline{40} \\ 6 \end{array}$$

15. Cups of coffee:

$8400 \div 100 = 84$

No. of rinses:

$84 \div 7 = 12$

$$\begin{array}{r} 12 \\ 7\overline{)84} \\ \underline{7} \\ 14 \\ \underline{14} \end{array}$$

The coffee filter needs to be rinsed 12 times before the machine is refilled.

16a. Gary: $1771 \div 8 = 221R3$

Ashley: $809 \div 4 = 202R1$

$$\begin{array}{r} 221R3 \\ 8\overline{)1771} \\ \underline{16} \\ 17 \\ \underline{16} \\ 11 \\ \underline{8} \\ 3 \end{array} \qquad \begin{array}{r} 202R1 \\ 4\overline{)809} \\ \underline{80} \\ 9 \\ \underline{8} \\ 1 \end{array}$$

Gary has more beans in each jar and more leftover beans.

b. Gary:

$221 \div 5 = 44R1$
$221 \div 6 = 36R5$
$221 \div 7 = 31R4$

Ashley:

$202 \div 5 = 40R2$
$202 \div 6 = 33R4$
$202 \div 7 = 28R6$

They must both have 4 beans left. Gary splits his beans into 7 piles and Ashley splits her beans into 6 piles.

17a. $1000 \div 1 = 1000$ $1000 \div 2 = 500$
$1000 \div 3 = 333R1$ $1000 \div 4 = 250$
$1000 \div 5 = 200$ $1000 \div 6 = 166R4$
$1000 \div 7 = 142R6$ $1000 \div 8 = 125$
$1000 \div 9 = 111R1$

Jason uses 6 vases.

b. Jason can use 1, 2, 4, 5, or 8 vases so that there are no leftover marbles.

18. $2000 \div 6 = 333R2$ $2000 \div 7 = 285R5$
$2000 \div 8 = 250$

8 potatoes in a bag will have no leftovers.

5 Fractions

Math Skills

1. (Suggested answers)

a. $\frac{2}{3}$; $\frac{4}{6}$ b. $\frac{2}{5}$; $\frac{4}{10}$ c. $\frac{1}{4}$; $\frac{2}{8}$

d. $2\frac{1}{3}$; $\frac{7}{3}$ e. $1\frac{1}{2}$; $1\frac{4}{8}$

2a. $\frac{3}{4}$ b. $\frac{4}{5}$ c. $\frac{7}{8}$

d. $\frac{6}{10}$ e. $\frac{4}{6}$ f. $\frac{5}{8}$

g. $1\frac{1}{2}$ h. $\frac{6}{5}$ i. $2\frac{3}{5}$

j. $3\frac{1}{3}$ k. $\frac{17}{3}$ l. $\frac{20}{7}$

3a. $\frac{1}{7}$, $\frac{3}{7}$, $\frac{4}{7}$, $\frac{5}{7}$ b. $\frac{1}{3}$, $\frac{5}{9}$, $\frac{6}{9}$, $\frac{4}{3}$

c. $\frac{3}{4}$, $\frac{7}{8}$, $\frac{5}{4}$, $1\frac{1}{2}$ d. $1\frac{1}{2}$, $\frac{14}{4}$, $\frac{17}{4}$, $\frac{9}{2}$

Problem Solving

$\frac{1}{8} < \frac{2}{8}$; Steve

1. Kayleen: $\frac{1}{6}$ Keith: $\frac{2}{6} = \frac{1}{3}$

Keith

2. Dave: $\frac{3}{4}$ Eric: $\frac{1}{2}$

$\frac{3}{4} > \frac{1}{2}$

Dave

3a. Miranda: $\frac{3}{5}$

Wilson: $\frac{7}{8}$

Wilson

b. Rachel: $\frac{6}{10}$

$\frac{6}{10} = \frac{3}{5}$

$\frac{6}{10} < \frac{7}{8}$

Wilson

4.

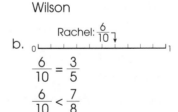

Andrew
5 slices left
Andrew's sister

$\frac{5}{8}$

5.

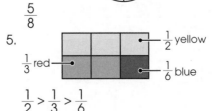

$\frac{1}{2}$ yellow
$\frac{1}{3}$ red
$\frac{1}{6}$ blue

$\frac{1}{2} > \frac{1}{3} > \frac{1}{6}$

Yellow ; blue

ISBN: 978-1-77149-202-7

6.

$\frac{5}{8}$ orange juice

$\frac{1}{4}$ lime juice

$\frac{1}{8}$ soda

$\frac{5}{8} > \frac{1}{4} > \frac{1}{8}$

orange juice

7a. pepperoni pizza

$\frac{2}{10}$

vegetarian pizza

$\frac{2}{6}$

$\frac{2}{6} > \frac{2}{10}$

Cynthia ate more of the vegetarian pizza.

b. Hawaiian pizza

$\frac{2}{8}$

$\frac{2}{10} < \frac{2}{8} < \frac{2}{6}$

Cynthia ate $\frac{2}{8}$ of the Hawaiian pizza.

8a.

$\frac{15}{6} = 2\frac{3}{6} = 2\frac{1}{2}$

$2\frac{1}{2}$ pizzas were sold.

b.

$2\frac{4}{6} > 2\frac{1}{2}$

More pizzas were sold yesterday.

9. Daniel: $1\frac{1}{2}$

Daniel's brother: $\frac{7}{6} = 1\frac{1}{6}$

$1\frac{1}{2} > 1\frac{1}{6}$

Daniel has read more.

10. $\frac{11}{5} < \frac{11}{3}$

Lisa ran more laps yesterday.

11a. $0 + 1 + 3 + 2 + 5 + 8 + 6 = 25$

$\frac{1}{25}$ of Teresa's friends voted for Tuesday.

b. $8 + 6 = 14$

$\frac{14}{25}$ of Teresa's friends voted for a weekend.

c. Saturday has $\frac{8}{25}$ of the votes.

d. $\frac{1}{5} = \frac{5}{25}$

Friday has $\frac{1}{5}$ of the votes.

12a. Green: $10 - 6 - 2 = 2$

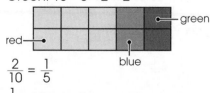

green

red

blue

$\frac{2}{10} = \frac{1}{5}$

$\frac{1}{5}$ of the balloons are green.

b. $6 + 2 = 8$

$\frac{8}{10} = \frac{4}{5}$

$\frac{4}{5}$ of the balloons are not green.

13. $20 - 6 = 14$

$\frac{14}{20} = \frac{7}{10}$

Lydia still has $\frac{7}{10}$ of her cookies.

14a.

$\frac{5}{6}$

$\frac{7}{8}$

$\frac{7}{8} > \frac{5}{6}$

$\frac{7}{8}$ of a prize is the better choice.

b.

$\frac{9}{10}$

$\frac{9}{10} > \frac{7}{8}$

Yes, Ben should give up his previous choice.

15. Bonnie: $\frac{13}{4} = 3\frac{1}{4}$ Donnie: $\frac{27}{8} = 3\frac{3}{8}$

Connie: $\frac{16}{6} = 2\frac{4}{6} = 2\frac{2}{3}$

$2\frac{2}{3} < 3\frac{1}{4} < 3\frac{3}{8}$

Connie crossed first, Bonnie crossed second, and Donnie crossed third.

16a. Evan: $\frac{77}{100}$ Sarah: $\frac{33}{50} = \frac{66}{100}$

$\frac{77}{100} > \frac{66}{100}$

Evan is closer to finishing the scavenger hunt.

b. Sarah: $66 + 12 = 78$

$\frac{78}{100} > \frac{77}{100}$

Sarah is closer to finishing the scavenger hunt now.

17a.

$2\frac{7}{10}$ g more $\frac{22}{7} = 3\frac{1}{7}$ g more

teddy bear   robot   doll

The doll weighs more.

b.

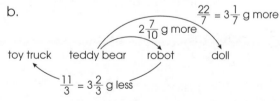

$\frac{22}{7} = 3\frac{1}{7}$ g more

$2\frac{7}{10}$ g more

toy truck   teddy bear   robot   doll

$\frac{11}{3} = 3\frac{2}{3}$ g less

The toys ordered from lightest to heaviest are toy truck, teddy bear, robot, and doll.

ISBN: 978-1-77149-202-7

6 Decimals

Math Skills

1. 1.2   2. 1.1   3. 1   4. 0.9
5. 0.4   6. 1.9   7. 7.9   8. 14.5
9. 12.3   10. 3.4   11. 2.8   12. 3.6
13. 11   14. 8.5   15. 12   16. 4.5
17. 9.2   18. 13.9   19. 4.5   20. 3.2
21. 9.5   22. 25.9   23. 3.1   24. 15.5

Problem Solving

2.2 ; 2 ; 2 ; 2.2

1. 0.6 + 0.8 = 1.4
   1.4

   $$\begin{array}{r} 0.6 \\ + \ 0.8 \\ \hline 1.4 \end{array}$$

2. 4.1 − 0.9 = 3.2
   3.2

   $$\begin{array}{r} 4.1 \\ - \ 0.9 \\ \hline 3.2 \end{array}$$

3a. 6.2 + 6.2 = 12.4
    12.4

   $$\begin{array}{r} 6.2 \\ + \ 6.2 \\ \hline 12.4 \end{array}$$

   b. Round trip by train: 4.9 + 4.9 = 9.8
      Difference: 12.4 − 9.8 = 2.6

   $$\begin{array}{r} 4.9 \\ + \ 4.9 \\ \hline 9.8 \end{array} \qquad \begin{array}{r} 12.4 \\ - \ 9.8 \\ \hline 2.6 \end{array}$$

      2.6

4. 2.1 + 1.6 + 1.9 = 5.6
   5.6

   $$\begin{array}{r} 2.1 \\ 1.6 \\ + \ 1.9 \\ \hline 5.6 \end{array}$$

5a. 7.8 + 2.7 = 10.5
    10.5

   $$\begin{array}{r} 7.8 \\ + \ 2.7 \\ \hline 10.5 \end{array}$$

   b. Third section: 7.8 − 1.9 = 5.9
      Entire trail: 7.8 + 10.5 + 5.9 = 24.2

   $$\begin{array}{r} 7.8 \\ - \ 1.9 \\ \hline 5.9 \end{array} \qquad \begin{array}{r} 7.8 \\ 10.5 \\ + \ 5.9 \\ \hline 24.2 \end{array}$$

      24.2

6a. 16.7 − 3.4 = 13.3
    Chris has climbed 13.3 m.

   $$\begin{array}{r} 16.7 \\ - \ 3.4 \\ \hline 13.3 \end{array}$$

   b. 16.7 − 6.9 = 9.8
      Chris needs to climb down
      9.8 m more.

   $$\begin{array}{r} 16.7 \\ - \ 6.9 \\ \hline 9.8 \end{array}$$

7a. 20.8 + 56.8 = 77.6
    The total capacity of
    Mr. Leung's aquariums is 77.6 L.

   $$\begin{array}{r} 20.8 \\ + \ 56.8 \\ \hline 77.6 \end{array}$$

   b. 94.6 − 77.6 = 17
      Mr. Leung can add 17 L more
      water to the new aquarium.

   $$\begin{array}{r} 94.6 \\ - \ 77.6 \\ \hline 17.0 \end{array}$$

8a. 17.3 − 2.7 = 14.6
    Randy threw 14.6 m last year.

   $$\begin{array}{r} 17.3 \\ - \ 2.7 \\ \hline 14.6 \end{array}$$

   b. 17.3 + 5.8 = 23.1
      The world record for
      shot put is 23.1 m.

   $$\begin{array}{r} 17.3 \\ + \ 5.8 \\ \hline 23.1 \end{array}$$

9a. 43.2 + 45.7 + 51.9 = 140.8
    Shawn's total time was
    140.8 seconds.

   $$\begin{array}{r} 43.2 \\ 45.7 \\ + \ 51.9 \\ \hline 140.8 \end{array}$$

   b. 140.8 − 38.5 − 44.6 = 57.7
      Beverly's time for the third lap
      was 57.7 seconds.

   $$\begin{array}{r} 140.8 \\ - \ 38.5 \\ \hline 102.3 \\ - \ 44.6 \\ \hline 57.7 \end{array}$$

10a. 3.5 − 0.7 − 0.7 − 0.7 = 1.4
     1.4 L of hand soap is left in
     the bag.

   $$\begin{array}{r} 3.5 \\ - \ 0.7 \\ \hline 2.8 \\ - \ 0.7 \\ \hline 2.1 \\ - \ 0.7 \\ \hline 1.4 \end{array}$$

   b. 3.1 − 1.4 = 1.7
      1.7 L of water is used.

   $$\begin{array}{r} 3.1 \\ - \ 1.4 \\ \hline 1.7 \end{array}$$

11. Louise's time: 21.6 + 1.9 = 23.5
    Nelson's time: 23.5 − 2.4 = 21.1

   $$\begin{array}{r} 21.6 \\ + \ 1.9 \\ \hline 23.5 \end{array} \qquad \begin{array}{r} 23.5 \\ - \ 2.4 \\ \hline 21.1 \end{array}$$

    Nelson's time was 21.1 min.

12a. Path A: 2.5 + 4.4 = 6.9
     Path B: 2.8 + 2.1 + 2.7 = 7.6

   $$\begin{array}{r} 2.5 \\ + \ 4.4 \\ \hline 6.9 \end{array} \qquad \begin{array}{r} 2.8 \\ 2.1 \\ + \ 2.7 \\ \hline 7.6 \end{array}$$

     Path A is shorter. It is 6.9 km long.

   b. 7.6 − 3.7 = 3.9
      The shortcut is 3.9 km long.

   $$\begin{array}{r} 7.6 \\ - \ 3.7 \\ \hline 3.9 \end{array}$$

13. 56.7 − 55.9 = 0.8
    The difference is 0.8 m.

   $$\begin{array}{r} 56.7 \\ - \ 55.9 \\ \hline 0.8 \end{array}$$

14a. Weight a truck can carry: 18.2 − 9.4 = 8.8
     2 trips: 8.8 + 8.8 = 17.6

   $$\begin{array}{r} 18.2 \\ - \ 9.4 \\ \hline 8.8 \end{array} \qquad \begin{array}{r} 8.8 \\ + \ 8.8 \\ \hline 17.6 \end{array}$$

     A truck can carry 17.6 tonnes in 2 trips.

   b. 17.6 + 17.6 + 17.6 + 17.6 = 70.4
      Yes, 4 trucks can carry 70 tonnes
      in 2 trips.

   $$\begin{array}{r} 17.6 \\ 17.6 \\ 17.6 \\ + \ 17.6 \\ \hline 70.4 \end{array}$$

15a. Scores in order: 6.3, 6.8, 7.2, 7.4, 7.6
     Total: 6.8 + 7.2 + 7.4 = 21.4
     Natalie's final score was 21.4.

   $$\begin{array}{r} 6.8 \\ 7.2 \\ + \ 7.4 \\ \hline 21.4 \end{array}$$

   b. Penalized score: 7.6 − 0.3 = 7.3
      New scores in order: 6.3, 6.8, 7.2, 7.3, 7.4
      New total: 6.8 + 7.2 + 7.3 = 21.3

   $$\begin{array}{r} 7.6 \\ - \ 0.3 \\ \hline 7.3 \end{array} \qquad \begin{array}{r} 6.8 \\ 7.2 \\ + \ 7.3 \\ \hline 21.3 \end{array}$$

      Natalie's final score would have been
      21.3.

ISBN: 978-1-77149-202-7

7 Money

Math Skills

1. 9.25 ; $20 ; $46.40 ; $181.30
2a. $9.25 ; $20 ; $29.25
   b. $20 + $46.40 = $66.40
   c. $20 + $181.30 = $201.30
   d. $46.40 + $181.30 = $227.70
3a. $46.40 ; $9.25 ; $37.15
   b. $46.40 – $20 = $26.40
   c. $181.30 – $20 = $161.30
   d. $181.30 – $46.40 = $134.90

Problem Solving

$69.70 ; 69.70 ; 69.70

1. $40.50 – $36.20 = $4.30
   4.30

   ```
     40.50
   – 36.20
     4.30
   ```

2. Leonard's savings: $42.45
   $50 – $42.45 = $7.55
   7.55

   ```
     50.00
   – 42.45
     7.55
   ```

3a. Freddie's savings: $56.40
   $56.40 + $7.30 = $63.70
   63.70

   ```
     56.40
   +  7.30
     63.70
   ```

   b. Freddie's money: $56.40 + $10 = $66.40
   Change: $66.40 – $63.70 = $2.70

   ```
     56.40          66.40
   + 10.00        – 63.70
     66.40           2.70
   ```

   2.70

4a. $11.25 + $11.25 + $8.60 = $31.10
   31.10

   ```
     11.25
     11.25
   +  8.60
     31.10
   ```

   b. $35 – $31.10 = $3.90
   Kyle's change: $3.70
   did not

   ```
     35.00
   – 31.10
      3.90
   ```

5. Total: $15.95 + $6.40 + $12.15 = $34.50
   Change: $50 – $34.50 = $15.50

   ```
     15.95          50.00
      6.40        – 34.50
   + 12.15          15.50
     34.50
   ```

   1 $10 bill, 1 $5 bill, and 2 quarters.

6a. Jeffrey: $36.25 – $8.45 = $27.80
   Craig: $27.90 + $8.45 = $36.35

   ```
     36.25          27.90
   –  8.45        +  8.45
     27.80          36.35
   ```

   Jeffrey has $27.80 and Craig has $36.35.

   b. $36.35 – $27.80 = $8.55
   Craig has $8.55 more than
   Jeffrey.

   ```
     36.35
   – 27.80
      8.55
   ```

7a. $47.75 – $19.90 = $27.85
   The sweater cost $27.85.

   ```
     47.75
   – 19.90
     27.85
   ```

b. 2 sweaters: $27.85 + $27.85 = $55.70
   Difference: $55.70 – $47.75 = $7.95

   ```
     27.85          55.70
   + 27.85        – 47.75
     55.70           7.95
   ```

   Judy would have paid $7.95 more.

8a. Audrey's money before:
   $48.95 – $24.70 = $24.25

   ```
     48.95
   – 24.70
     24.25
   ```

   Audrey's money after:
   $24.25 + $1.35 = $25.60
   Audrey has $25.60 now.

   ```
     24.25
   +  1.35
     25.60
   ```

   b. Santos's money:
   $74.45 – $48.95 = $25.50
   No, Audrey has more money.

   ```
     74.45
   – 48.95
     25.50
   ```

9a. DVD: $34.75 – $21.60 = $13.15
   Video game: $45.20 – $32.65 = $12.55

   ```
     34.75          45.20
   – 21.60        – 32.65
     13.15          12.55
   ```

   The DVD has a bigger price reduction.

   b. $13.15 + $12.55 = $25.70
   Bobby will save $25.70
   in total.

   ```
     13.15
   + 12.55
     25.70
   ```

10. Regular movie ticket:
   $16.45 – $3.15 = $13.30

   ```
     16.45
   –  3.15
     13.30
   ```

   2 regular movie tickets:
   $13.30 + $13.30 = $26.60

   ```
     13.30
   + 13.30
     26.60
   ```

   2 regular movie tickets will cost $26.60.

11. Gas: $78.20 – $34.75 = $43.45
   Difference: $43.45 – $34.75 = $8.70

   ```
     78.20          43.45
   – 34.75        – 34.75
     43.45           8.70
   ```

   $8.70 more was spent on gas than on snacks.

12. 5 $20 = $100
   Jenny's remaining money:
   $100 – $37.15 = $62.85

   ```
    100.00
   – 37.15
     62.85
   ```

   Total cost of items:
   $45.10 + $33.20 = $78.30

   ```
     45.10
   + 33.20
     78.30
   ```

   Difference:
   $78.30 – $62.85 = $15.45

   ```
     78.30
   – 62.85
     15.45
   ```

   Jenny needs $15.45 more.

13a. Penelope: $48.80
   Total: $36.75 + $48.80 = $85.55
   Ella and Penelope have $85.55
   together.

   ```
     36.75
   + 48.80
     85.55
   ```

   b. Cost of 3 cakes:
   $28.50 + $28.50 + $28.50
   = $85.50

   ```
     28.50
     28.50
   + 28.50
     85.50
   ```

   Yes, they have enough money.

ISBN: 978-1-77149-202-7

14. Elizabeth's earnings:
$11.80 + $11.80 + $11.80 = $35.40
Jonathan's earnings:
$12.15 + $12.15 = $24.30
Difference:
$35.40 − $24.30 = $11.10

```
   11.80          12.15          35.40
   11.80        + 12.15        − 24.30
 + 11.80          24.30          11.10
   35.40
```

The difference between their earnings is $11.10.

15. $55 − $15.35 − $15.35 − $15.35 = $8.95

```
   55.00
 − 15.35
   39.65
 − 15.35
   24.30
 − 15.35
    8.95
```

Ms. Johnson can buy 3 notebooks and she will have $8.95 left.

16. Total cost: $18.75 + $14.05 + $22.30 = $55.10
Amount paid: $55.10 + $4.90 = $60

```
   18.75          55.10
   14.05        +  4.90
 + 22.30          60.00
   55.10
```

$60 = [$20] [$10]
Mr. McNeil paid using 2 $20 bills and 2 $10 bills.

17. Cost of buying: $45.95 − $15.50 = $30.45
Cost of renting:
$4.50 + $4.50 + $4.50 + $4.50 = $18

```
   45.95           4.50
 − 15.50           4.50
   30.45           4.50
                 + 4.50
                  18.00
```

Bernard should rent skates.

18. Paula's remaining money:
$100 − $56.25 − $29.15 = $14.60
Spending on muffins:
$4.55 + $4.55 + $4.55 = $13.65

```
  100.00           4.55
 − 56.25           4.55
   43.75         + 4.55
 − 29.15          13.65
   14.60
```

Paula can buy 3 muffins.

8 Time

Math Skills

1. 120	2. 4	3. 240
4. 10	5. 21	6. 18
7. 3	8. 540	9. 156
10. 50	11. 120	12. 30

13a. 10:30 ; 11:45 ; 1 h 15 min
b. 8:45 ; 11:15 ; 2 h 30 min
c. 1 h 43 min   d. 4 h 25 min
e. 12   f. 55
g. 4   h. 3

Problem Solving

0:50 ; 50
1. Elapsed time: 45 min
End time: 7:05 p.m.
6:20 p.m.

```
  6 7:05 65
 −   0:45
    6:20
```

2a. Start time: 6:40 p.m.
End time: 8:15 p.m.
1 h 35 min

```
  7 8:15 75
 −   6:40
    1:35
```

b. Start time: 11:35 a.m.
Elapsed time: 2 h 15 min
13:50 = 1:50 p.m.
1:50 p.m.

```
   11:35
 +  2:15
   13:50
```

3. Start time: 9:32 a.m.
End time: 2:16 p.m. = 14:16
4 h 44 min

```
  13 14:16 76
 −    9:32
     4:44
```

4. 1 lesson: 45 min
8 lessons: 45 × 8 = 360
360 minutes = 6 hours
6 hours

```
    45
 ×   8
   360
```

5a. Elapsed time: 3 h 30 min
End time: 12:00 p.m.
8:30 a.m.

```
  11 12:00 60
 −    3:30
     8:30
```

b. Start time: 00:00
Elapsed time: 1 h 15 min
1:15 a.m.

```
   00:00
 +  1:15
    1:15
```

6a. Start time: 5:30 p.m.
Elapsed time: 2 h 20 min
Arrival time: 7:50 p.m.
Yes, Ana will arrive before the concert starts.

```
    5:30
 +  2:20
    7:50
```

b. 15 min before concert:
Elapsed time: 15 min
End time: 7:55 p.m.
Time to leave:
Elapsed time: 2 h 20 min
End time: 7:40 p.m.
Ana should leave at 5:20 p.m.

```
    7:55
 −  0:15
    7:40
```

```
    7:40
 −  2:20
    5:20
```

7. End of yoga class:
Start time: 7:30 a.m.
Elapsed time: 55 min
End time: 8:25 a.m.
Kendra's arrival time:
Elapsed time: 45 min
End time: 8:25 a.m.
Arrival time: 7:40 a.m.
Kendra arrived at 7:40 a.m.

```
    7:30
 +  0:55
  8 7:85 25
```

```
  7 8:25 85
 −   0:45
    7:40
```

8.

```
   May            June
  28 29 30 31  1  2  3  4  5  6  7  8  9  10
   1  2  3  4  5  6  7  8  9 10 11 12 13
```

Patsy will be on the cruise for 13 days.

9a. Hours on a weekday:
   Start time: 8:00 a.m.
   End time: 7:30 p.m. = 19:30

$$\begin{array}{r} 19{:}30 \\ -\ 8{:}00 \\ \hline 11{:}30 \end{array}$$

   Hours on weekends:
   Elapsed time: 2 h 30 min
   Hours on a weekday: 11 h 30 min

$$\begin{array}{r} 11{:}30 \\ -\ 2{:}30 \\ \hline 9{:}00 \end{array}$$

   The library is open for 9 hours a day on weekends.

b. Hours on weekdays:
   11 h 30 min × 5
   = 55 h 150 min
   = 57 h 30 min
   Hours on the weekend: 9 × 2 = 18
   Total: 57 h 30 min + 18 h = 75 h 30 min
   The library is open for 75 h 30 min in a week.

10a. Wednesdays:
   Mar. 9, Mar. 16, Mar. 23, Mar. 30, Apr. 6, Apr. 13, Apr. 20, Apr. 27, May 4
   There were 9 classes.

b. Class dates of 9 classes:
   Dec. 14, Dec. 7, Nov. 30, Nov. 23, Nov. 16, Nov. 9, Nov. 2, Oct. 26, Oct. 19
   The program begins in October.

11. Non-leap year: 365 days
   Leap year: 366 days
   There are at most 3 leap years in a decade.
   3 leap years: 366 × 3 = 1098
   7 non-leap years: 365 × 7 = 2555
   1098 + 2555 = 3653
   At most, there are 3653 days in a decade.

12. Start time: May 1, 2016

```
      12 months      12 months      6 months
May 1, 2016   May 1, 2017   May 1, 2018   Nov. 1, 2018
```

   Roberta's lease would end on November 1, 2018.

13. Start time: Nov. 10

```
     1 week   1 week   1 week   2 days
  Oct. 18  Oct. 25  Nov. 1  Nov. 8  Nov. 10
```

   The quiz was on October 18.

14a. Next scan: Sep. 7
   Today: Aug. 14
   From Aug. 14 to Aug. 31 = 17 days
   From Aug. 31 to Sep. 6 = 6 days
   17 + 6 = 23
   There are 23 days until the next scan.

b. End of the year: Dec. 31
   Days of 7th between Aug. 14 and Dec. 31:
   Sep. 7, Oct. 7, Nov. 7, Dec. 7
   There will be 4 scans.

15a. Start time:
   Nov. 11, 11:10 p.m. = Nov. 11, 23:10
   Elapsed time:
   1 h 35 min + 2 h 25 min = 4 h

$$\begin{array}{r} 23{:}10 \\ +\ 4{:}00 \\ \hline 27{:}10 \end{array}$$

   Nov. 11, 27:10 = Nov. 12, 3:10 a.m.
   Vernon arrives on Nov. 12 at 3:10 a.m.

b. Elapsed time: 4 h – 1 h 45 min = 2 h 15 min
   End time: Nov. 18, 1:30 a.m.

```
Nov. 17        25
  Nov. 18    1:30
 −           2:15
  Nov. 17  23:15
```

   23:15 = 11:15 p.m.
   Vernon departs on Nov. 17 at 11:15 p.m.

16. Start time:
   Oct. 29, 5:40 p.m. = Oct. 29, 17:40
   Elapsed time:
   3 h 10 min + 15 h = 18 h 10 min

```
   Oct. 29      17:40
 +             18:10
   Oct. 29     35:50
        30  11
```

   The earliest time Greta can start the 2nd coat is on Oct. 30 at 11:50 p.m.

17a. Start time: Apr. 25, 2:35 p.m.
   End time: Apr. 27, 5:20 p.m.

```
              4    80
   Apr. 27   5:20 p.m.
 − Apr. 25   2:35 p.m.
        2    2:45
```

   Elapsed time: 2 days 2 h 45 min
   It took 2 days, 2 hours, and 45 minutes for Susan's book to arrive.

b. Start time: Apr. 29, 11:25 a.m.
   Elapsed time: 2 days 2 h 45 min

```
   Apr. 29     11:25
 +     2       2:45
   Apr. 31     13:70
 May 1      14    10
```

   May 1, 14:10 = May 1, 2:10 p.m.
   The book should arrive on May 1 at 2:10 p.m.

9 Perimeter and Area

Math Skills

1. A: 12 ; 9   B: 12 cm ; 8 cm²
   C: 24 cm ; 11 cm²   D: 16 cm ; 8 cm²
   E: 17 cm ; 8.5 cm²   F: 15 cm ; 9.5 cm²
2. 32 m ; 64 m²   3. 44 cm ; 105 cm²
4. 14 m ; 6 m²

ISBN: 978-1-77149-202-7

Problem Solving

12 ; 12

1. 20 + 20 + 15 + 15 = 70

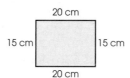

70

2. Chocolate cookie: 3 + 3 + 3 + 3 + 3 = 15
Gingerbread cookie: 3 + 3 + 4 + 4 = 14
Sesame cookie: 4 + 4 + 4 = 12
chocolate cookie

3. 12 + 12 + 15 + 15 = 54

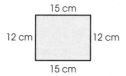

54

4. 23 + 23 + 23 + 23 = 92

92

5. 50 + 50 + 60 + 60 = 220
220

6. 2.6 m = 260 cm
260 + 260 + 60 + 60 = 640

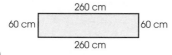

640

7. 1450 + 1450 + 1450 + 1450 = 5800
5800 cm = 58 m = 0.058 km

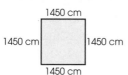

0.058

8. Perimeter: 12 000 cm = 120 m
Total width: 120 − 50 − 50 = 20
Width: 20 ÷ 2 = 10
The width of the pool is 10 m.

9. 100 + 100 + 100 + 100 + 65 + 65 = 530

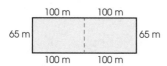

530 m of fencing is needed for both patches of land.

10a. Stamp A: 4 + 4 + 3 + 3 = 14
Stamp B: 3 + 3 + 5 + 5 = 16
Lisa's favourite stamp is Stamp B.

 b. Stamp A: 4 × 3 = 12
Stamp B: 3 × 5 = 15
Stamp B was used.

11a. 3 × 13 = 39
No, one bucket of paint will not be enough.

 b.

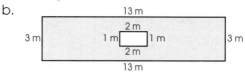

Area of window: 2 × 1 = 2
Area of wall with window: 39 − 2 = 37
Yes, one bucket of paint will be enough.

12a. 8 × 6 = 48

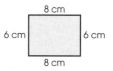

The area of the photo is 48 cm².

 b. Thomas needs to consider the dimensions of the photo as well. The frame's width is shorter than the photo's width, so the photo cannot fit.

13a. Perimeter of Tablecloth A:
203 + 203 + 95 + 95 = 596
Perimeter of Tablecloth B:
210 + 210 + 90 + 90 = 600

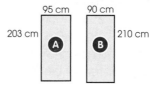

Emily sewed the fringe onto the tablecloth measuring 210 cm by 90 cm.

 b. Area of Tablecloth A: 203 × 95 = 19 285
Area of Tablecloth B: 210 × 90 = 18 900
Emily used the tablecloth measuring 203 cm by 95 cm.

14a. Side length: 320 ÷ 4 = 80

Area: 80 × 80 = 6400
The area of the table when the pull-out is hidden is 6400 cm².

ISBN: 978-1-77149-202-7

b.
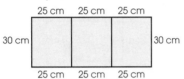

New length: 80 + 30 = 110
New area: 110 × 80 = 8800
The area of the table when it is extended
with the pull-out is 8800 cm².

15. Rectangles with a Perimeter of 12 cm

Length (cm)	Width (cm)	Area (cm²)
1	5	1 × 5 = 5
2	4	2 × 4 = 8
3	3	3 × 3 = 9 ← greatest
4	2	4 × 2 = 8
5	1	5 × 1 = 5

The dimensions of the frame should be
3 cm by 3 cm.

16a.
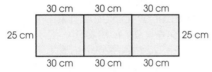

Perimeter: 25 × 6 = 150
            30 × 2 = 60
        150 + 60 = 210
The perimeter of his new canvas is 210 cm.

b.
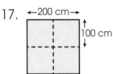

Perimeter: 30 × 6 = 180
            25 × 2 = 50
        180 + 50 = 230
Difference in perimeter: 230 – 210 = 20
The perimeter will be 20 cm longer.

17.

Original trimming: 200 × 4 = 800
Perimeter of 1 square: 100 × 4 = 400
Trimming needed: 400 × 4 = 1600
Difference in trimming: 1600 – 800 = 800
Sally needs 800 cm more trimming.

18a. Extending the length:
     Length: 5 + 3 = 8
     Area: 8 × 3 = 24

Extending the width:
Width: 3 + 3 = 6
Area: 5 × 6 = 30
Janelle should extend the
width of the garden.

b.
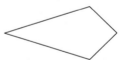

Original fencing: 5 + 5 + 3 + 3 = 16
New fencing: 5 + 5 + 6 + 6 = 22
Difference in fencing: 22 – 16 = 6
Janelle needs 6 m more fencing.

10 Shapes and Solids

Math Skills

1. A: square ; 4 ; 4 ; 2 pairs ; 4
   B: kite ; 0 ; 2 pairs ; 0 ; 1
   C: parallelogram ; 0 ; 2 pairs ; 2 pairs ; 0
   D: rectangle ; 4 ; 2 pairs ; 2 pairs ; 2
2. E: cube ; 6 ; 8 ; 12
   F: rectangular pyramid ; 5 ; 5 ; 8
   G: triangular prism ; 5 ; 6 ; 9
   H: rectangular prism ; 6 ; 8 ; 12

Problem Solving

square
1. Quadrilaterals with 2 pairs of parallel sides:

square   rectangle   parallelogram   rhombus

square, a rectangle, a parallelogram, or
a rhombus
2a. (Suggested drawing)

kite
b. A kite has one pair of angles opposite of
   each other that are equal.
3a. Yes, Joseph is correct.
b. No, Joyce is incorrect. This is a closed
   shape with 4 sides, so it is a quadrilateral.
4a. (Suggested answers)
    A: 4 equal sides   B: no right angles
    C: exactly 2 lines of symmetry
b. Only Shape B has angles that are bigger
   than a right angle.
   parallelogram
5. (Suggested drawing and answer)

        or

kite   trapezoid
Yes, the shape is a kite/trapezoid.

ISBN: 978-1-77149-202-7

6a.

	Front View	Top View	Side View

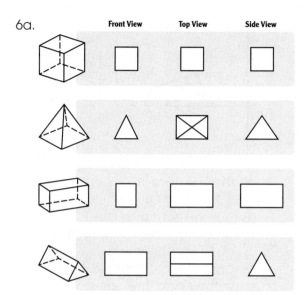

c.

It is a triangular pyramid. It has 4 faces, 4 vertices, and 6 edges.

d.

It is a triangular prism. It has 5 faces, 6 vertices, and 9 edges.

e. Alvin's solid has no right angles on any of its faces.

12.

triangular prism   triangular pyramid

Alycia's solids are a triangular prism and a triangular pyramid. They have 6 and 5 vertices respectively.

13. Francis's net cannot fold into a cube. Ernie's and Greta's nets are correct.

14. 1 triangular pyramid: 4 vertices, 6 edges
2 triangular pyramids: 8 vertices, 12 edges
3 triangular pyramids: 12 vertices, 18 edges
Ivan can construct 2 triangular pyramids.

15. The net makes a triangular prism, which has 9 edges. Naysha needs 9 sticks.

16. Octagonal pyramid: 9 vertices, 16 edges
Rectangular prism: 8 vertices, 12 edges
No. of balls: 9 – 8 = 1
No. of sticks: 16 – 12 = 4
4 sticks and 1 ball are left.

b. The cube's views are identical. It has 6 faces, 8 vertices, and 12 edges.

7-12. (Suggested drawings)

7.

Karson needs to paint 6 faces.

8.

Renée needs to smooth out 8 corners.

9.

Eric stacked cylinders.

10.

It is a triangular pyramid.

11a.

It is a rectangular pyramid. It has 5 faces, 5 vertices, and 8 edges.

b.

It is a rectangular prism. It has 6 faces, 8 vertices, and 12 edges.

11 Locations and Movements

Math Skills

1a. translation   b. reflection
c. rotation   d. reflection
e. rotation   f. translation

2. 🐶(1,10) 🐸(7,10) 🐰(8,8) 🐱(2,8)
🐟(5,6) 🐙(8,2) 🐭(3,3) 🐨(1,2)

Problem Solving

4 ; 2 ; 4 ; 2

1a. 5 units down ; 1 unit to the right
b. 5 units to the left ; 4 units up
2a. cafe: (1,7)   park: (3,5)   school:(8,2)
mall: (10,5)   pool: (7,7)   library: (5,2)

ISBN: 978-1-77149-202-7

b.

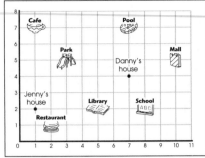

c. 1 unit to the right and 2 units down
d. 3 units to the left
e. 2 units to the right and 5 units up
f. mall
g. cafe ; 9 units to the left and 2 units up
h. 6 units to the left
i. 2 units to the right and 3 units down
j. 2 units to the right and 2 units down to the park. Then she went 2 units to the left and 3 units down to her home

3a.

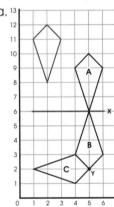

b. A: (4,9), (5,10), (5,6), (6,9)
B: (4,3), (5,2), (5,6), (6,3)
C: (1,2), (4,3), (4,1), (5,2)
c. Andrew coloured Image C.
d. Image A has the ink blot on it.
e. The coordinates (5,5), (5,4), and (5,3) are covered.

4a.

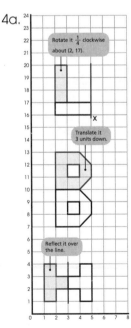

b. The letters are L, B, and H.
c. B ; L ; H ; none ; B
(Suggested answers)
d. Reflect L over Line X.
e. Rotate H $\frac{1}{4}$ clockwise about (5,1).

5a.

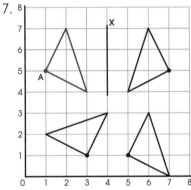

b. A to X: Rotate it $\frac{1}{4}$ clockwise about Point O.
A to Y: Reflect it over Line P.
A to Z: Translate it 7 units to the right and 3 units down.
c. Swapped coordinates: (6,4), (3,5), (3,2)

6a. Yes, they had the same coordinates because making a $\frac{1}{2}$ rotation clockwise and counterclockwise results in the same image.
b. The dots are 2 units horizontally and 2 units vertically apart.

7.

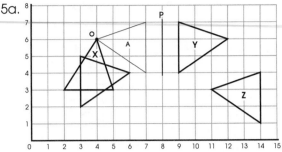

a. Point A will translate 6 units to the right.
b. Point A will translate 2 units to the right and 4 units down.
c. The coordinates of Point A will be (5,1).

12 Patterning and Equations

Math Skills

1. A: 32 ; 64
2 ; 2
B: 7 ; 12
Start at 3. Add 3. Then subtract 1.
C: 18 ; 33 ; 66
Start at 5. Multiply by 2. Then subtract 1.

ISBN: 978-1-77149-202-7

D: 24 ; 23 ; 68

Start at 4. Subtract 1. Then multiply by 3.

2. 4	3. 7	4. 5
5. 4	6. 26	7. 1
8. 6	9. 8	10. 4
11. 30	12. 2	13. 3

Problem Solving

11 ; 13 ; 13

1.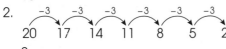
3   6   9   12   15   18

18

2.
20   17   14   11   8   5   2

2

3a. Week: 1   2   3   4   5   6   7
Stickers: 2   3   4   5   6   7   8

8

b. $2 + 3 + 4 + 5 + 6 + 7 + 8 = 35$

35

4a.
Day	Pattern
1	+1
2	−2
3	+3
4	−4
5	+5
6	−6
7	+7

b.
Day	Pattern	No. of Cards
0	–	2
1	+1	3
2	−2	1
3	+3	4
4	−4	0

4

buy 7 cards

5. 1st: 4   2nd: $4 \times 2 - 3 = 5$
3rd: $5 \times 2 - 3 = 7$ 4th: $7 \times 2 - 3 = 11$
5th: $11 \times 2 - 3 = 19$ 6th: $19 \times 2 - 3 = 35$

35

6a. Start at 10 and increase by 2 the next day.
Then double the increase each day.

b.
   Mon   Tue   Wed   Thu   Fri   Sat   Sun
     +2   +4   +8   +16   +32   +64
   10   12   16   24   40   72   136

Mr. Foster will do 136 push-ups on Sunday.

7a.
   noon   1:00   2:00   3:00   4:00   5:00   6:00
     +4   ÷2   +4   ÷2   +4   ÷2
   20   24   12   16   8   12   6

Ivy will plant 6 flowers at 6:00.

b.
   noon   1:00   2:00   3:00   4:00
     +4   ÷2   +4   ÷2
   12   16   8   12   6

Ivy will plant 6 flowers at 4:00.

8. 13 ; 13 cupcakes were sold.

9. $p + 3 = 16 + 11$ 10. $56 \div t = 4 \times 2$
    $p + 3 = 27$ $56 \div t = 8$
       $p = 24$ $t = 7$
Ken has 24 pens.   There are 7 tables.

11. $b - 12 = 8 \times 11$
   $b - 12 = 88$
        $b = 100$
Ronald started with 100 buns.

12. $35 - 27 + b = 42$
        $8 + b = 42$
            $b = 34$
Ray added back 34 books.

13. $9 \times p = 53 + 46$
   $9 \times p = 99$
        $p = 11$
There were 11 Popsicles in each package.

14. $5 \times s = 47 - 7$
   $5 \times s = 40$
        $s = 8$
8 seeds were planted in each pot.

15. $5 \times f = 52 - 17$
   $5 \times f = 35$
        $f = 7$
There are 7 friends.

16. $15 \times s = 180 - 60$
   $15 \times s = 120$
         $s = 8$
There are 8 bags of small seashells.

17a. $5p + p = 270$
        $p = 45$
There are 45 edge pieces.

b. Non-edge pieces: $270 - 45 = 225$
   $56 + 56 + 7 + g = 225$
        $119 + g = 225$
            $g = 106$
There are 106 green pieces.

18a. $8 \times c = 168$
       $c = 21$
Lisa should bake 21 cheesecakes.

b. Each hour, 8 more slices are sold.

Hour	0	1	2	3	4	5	6
No. of Slices	168	160	144	120	88	48	0

(arrows: −8, −16, −24, −32, −40, −48)

It will take 6 hours to sell all the cheesecakes.

19. Each layer uses 5 fewer straws.

Layer	1	2	3	4	5	6	7
Straws	70	65	60	55	50	45	40

(arrows: −5, −5, −5, −5, −5, −5)

$18 + s = 40$
     $s = 22$
Esme will use 22 more straws to finish it.

ISBN: 978-1-77149-202-7

13 Data Management and Probability

Math Skills

1.

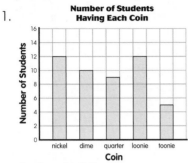

Number of Students Having Each Coin

2a. 1 ; 1 out of 2
  b. 1 out of 6 ; 1 out of 6
  c. 1 out of 4 ; 1 out of 4

Problem Solving

10 ; 12

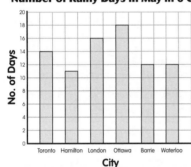

5 ; 5

2. **Number of Rainy Days in May in 6 Cities**

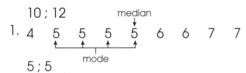

a. Ottawa has the most rainy days. ;
   Hamilton has the fewest rainy days.
b. No. of rainy days: 31 – 20 = 11
   Hamilton has 20 non-rainy days. ;
   No. of rainy days: 31 – 13 = 18
   Ottawa has 13 non-rainy days.
c. 11   12   12   14   16   18
         (12 + 14) ÷ 2 = 13
   13
d. 11   12   12   14   16   18
            mode
   12 ; Barrie and Waterloo
e. Yes. The mode number of non-rainy days is
   19 and the cities are Barrie and Waterloo.
 f. London: 31 – 16 = 15
   The difference between the number of
   rainy days and non-rainy days is 1.
   London

3a. On Wednesdays: 6   7   10   13   14
                                   median
The median sales on Wednesdays is $10.
On Fridays: 9   12   14   15
         (12 + 14) ÷ 2 = 13
The median sales on Fridays is $13.

b.

Day	Total Sales
Sun	$90
Mon	$30
Tue	$60
Wed	$50
Thu	$65
Fri	$50
Sat	$95

Sales of Lemonade in July

c. Saturday has the most sales. ;
   Monday has the least sales.
d. No, because there were 5 Tuesdays
   compared to only 4 Fridays, so it cannot
   be concluded that lemonade sells better
   on a Tuesday than a Friday by comparing
   the total sales.
e. It is unlikely that total sales on Mondays
   will exceed total sales on Sundays.
 f. Tue: The probability is 1 out of 7.
   Mon or Fri: The probability is 2 out of 7.
   Weekday: The probability is 5 out of 7.
   Weekend: The probability is 2 out of 7.
4a. Even numbers: 1̶ 2 3̶ 4 5̶ 6
   The probability is 3 out of 6.
   Numbers less than 4: 1 2 3 4̶ 5̶ 6̶
   The probability is 3 out of 6.
   Numbers that are not 5: 1 2 3 4 5̶ 6
   The probability is 5 out of 6.
  b. • Rolling a 3: 1 out of 6
     Rolling a no. greater than 3: 3 out of 6
     It is more likely to roll a number greater
     than 3.
   • Rolling a no. greater than 1: 5 out of 6
     Rolling a no. less than 2: 1 out of 6
     It is more likely to roll a number greater
     than 1.
  c. Rolling a 1 on a 6-sided dice: 1 out of 6
     Rolling a 1 on an 8-sided dice: 1 out of 8
     The probability of rolling a 1 would be less
     than Tom's dice.

5.

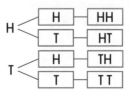

ISBN: 978-1-77149-202-7

a. There are 4 possible outcomes.
b. The possible outcomes are HH, HT, TH, and T T.
c. Flipping 2 heads: 1 out of 4
   Flipping at least 1 tail: 3 out of 4
d. Flipping 2 tails: 1 out of 4
   Flipping a head and a tail: 2 out of 4
   It is more likely to flip a head and a tail.

Critical-thinking Questions

Unit 1

1. 540 ; 280 ; 820 ; 820 ; 5 ; 4100 ; 4100 mL
2. (Suggested answer)
   $1.6 + 1.6 + 1.6 = 4.8$
   The total length of the 3 sides must be less than 4.8 cm.
   $8 - 4.8 = 3.2$ ← The 4th side is longer than 3.2 cm.
   The length of the 4th side is 3.3 cm.
3. There are 7 hours from 3 p.m. to 10 p.m.
   So, there will be 2 showings at most.
   Amount earned: $1623 + $1623 = $3246
   The theatre will earn $3246 at most.
4. Number of brownies: $16 \times 18 = 288$
   Number of bags: $288 \div 9 = 32$
   Bosco needs 32 bags.
5. Side length: $252 \div 4 = 63$
   Total length: $63 \times 12 = 756$
   The total length of all the edges is 756 cm.
6. Elle needs to walk 5 "200 m".
   Time needed: $3 \times 5 = 15$
   It takes Elle 15 min to get home.
7.

Square	Side Length (cm)	Area (cm²)
1	30 ⎫+20	900
2	50 ⎬+20	2500
3	70 ⎭	4900

   Total: $900 + 2500 + 4900 = 8300$
   The total area of the squares is 8300 cm².
8. Amount left: $1 - 0.6 - 0.2 = 0.2$

   $$0.2 = \frac{2}{10} = \frac{1}{5}$$ (÷2)

   $\frac{1}{5}$ of the box of chocolate is left.
9. Length of rectangle: $168 \div 4 = 42$
   Width of rectangle: $42 \div 2 = 21$
   Area: $42 \times 21 = 882$

21 cm 21 cm
42 cm

   The area of each rectangle is 882 cm².

10. Area of square: $3 \times 3 = 9$
    Number of squares: $882 \div 9 = 98$
    Tiffany will make 98 squares.
11.

Year	Distance (km)
2011	5 ⎫+0.5
2012	5.5 ⎬+0.5
2013	6
2014	6.5
2015	7

    Blake ran 0.5 km more every year.
    Total distance: $5 + 5.5 + 6 + 6.5 + 7 = 30$
    Blake had run 30 km by the end of 2015.
12. 13 $20 bills: $20 \times 13 = $260
    7 $5 bills: $5 \times 7 = $35
    Total amount: $260 + $35 = $295
    Area of fabric: $12 \times 2 = 24$
    Cost of fabric: $12 \times 24 = $288
    Amount left: $295 - $288 = $7
    Liam will have $7 left.
13. The length of 2 sides are 40.5 cm.

40.5 cm
40.5 cm

    Sum of other 2 sides: $183 - 40.5 - 40.5 = 102$
    Length of 1 other side: $102 \div 2 = 51$
    The lengths of the other 3 sides are 40.5 cm, 51 cm, and 51 cm.
14. 2 loonies: $2   1 quarter: $0.25
    5 nickels: $0.25
    Amount inserted: $2 + $0.25 + $0.25 = $2.50
    There are 10 $0.25 in $2.50.
    Time paid: $6 \times 10 = 60$
    Time needed: from 1:32 to 2:44 = 72 min
    Time to be paid: $72 - 60 = 12$
    Every 6 minutes costs $0.25. So, 12 minutes cost $0.50.
    $0.50 more is needed.
15.

Day	Distance (km)
1	2.7 ⎫+0.6
2	3.3
3	3.9
4	4.5 ← median
5	5.1
6	5.7
7	6.3

    The median distance Sandra runs in the first week is 4.5 km.
16. No. of 3-minute intervals: $45 \div 3 = 15$
    No. of units to the right: $3 \times 15 = 45$
    No. of units up: $2 \times 15 = 30$
    45 units to the right and 30 units up of (2,4) is (47,34).
    The car will be at (47,34) after 45 minutes.

ISBN: 978-1-77149-202-7

17.

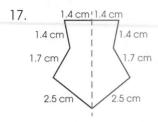

Perimeter:
$1.4 + 1.4 + 1.7 + 2.5 + 1.4 + 1.4 + 1.7 + 2.5 = 14$
The perimeter of the stamp is 14 cm.

18.

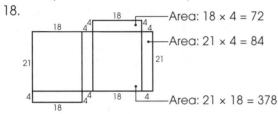

Area: $18 \times 4 = 72$
Area: $21 \times 4 = 84$
Area: $21 \times 18 = 378$

Perimeter:	Area:
$4 \times 8 = 32$	$72 \times 2 = 144$
$18 \times 4 = 72$	$84 \times 2 = 168$
$21 \times 2 = 42$	$378 \times 2 = 756$
$32 + 72 + 42 = 146$	$144 + 168 + 756 = 1068$

The perimeter is 146 cm and the area is 1068 cm².

19. 1 1 1 2 2 2 2 2 2
    3 3 3 3 ③ ③ 3 3 3 3
    4 4 4 4 4 5 5 5 5 6
Median: 3
There are 30 words in total and 10 words have 3 letters.
Fraction of words with 3 letters: $\frac{10}{30} = \frac{1}{3}$
$\frac{1}{3}$ of the words have the median number of letters.

20.

Shape	More than 1 line of symmetry	At least 1 pair of parallel sides
▭	✔	✔
▭	✔	✔
▱		✔
◇	✔	✔
⬠		✔
◇		

Probability: 3 out of 6   Probability: 5 out of 6
She is more likely to pick a shape with at least 1 pair of parallel sides.

Unit 2

1. $1.50 ; $1.50 ; $3 ; $3 ; 7 ; $21 ; $21
2. 2 $5 bills: $10   3 toonies: $6
   1 loonie: $1
   Total amount: $10 + $6 + $1 = $17
   No. of boards: $17 × 2 = 34
                        ↑
            Every $1 buys 2 boards.

No. of cubes: $34 \div 6 = 5R4$
                    ↑
            1 cube needs 6 boards.
Joel can afford to make 5 cubes.

3.

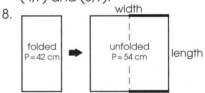

Perimeter: $9 + 12 + 15 + 9 + 6 + 3 = 54$
Total cost: $32 × 54 = $1728
It will cost Alexis $1728 to build her fence.

4. Watching TV: 20   Reading: 10
   Playing sports: 18   Singing: 12
   Total: $20 + 10 + 18 + 12 = 60$
   Fraction of friends who chose singing:
   $\frac{12}{60} = \frac{1}{5}$
   $\frac{1}{5}$ of Tyler's friends chose singing.

5. Watching TV or playing sports: $20 + 18 = 38$
   The probability is 38 out of 60.

6. 24 dozen: $24 × 12 = 288$
   Equation: $8d = 288$
   $d = 36$
   1 piece of dough makes 36 doughnuts.

7. Pattern rule: Each star moves 1 unit to the right and 2 units up.
   Coordinates:
   $+1 \big((1,1) \big) +2$
   $+1 \big((2,3) \big) +2$
   $+1 \big((3,5) \big) +2$
   $+1 \big((4,7) \big) +2$
   $\big((5,9) \big)$
   The coordinates of the next 2 stars are (4,7) and (5,9).

8.

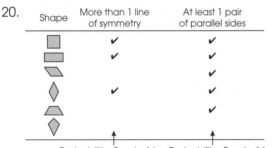

The difference in perimeter is the 2 widths that are in bold.
Difference: $54 - 42 = 12$
Unfolded width: $12 \div 2 \times 2 = 12$
Sum of 2 lengths: $54 - 12 - 12 = 30$
Length: $30 \div 2 = 15$
Area: $15 \times 12 = 180$
The area of the pamphlet when unfolded is 180 cm².

9.

Shape	Side Length (cm)
triangle	2.5
square	3
pentagon	3.5
hexagon	4
heptagon	4.5
octagon	5

(+0.5)

ISBN: 978-1-77149-202-7

The number of sides in a shape increases by 1 each time. The side lengths increase by 0.5 cm each time.
A regular octagon has 8 equal sides.
Perimeter: $5 \times 8 = 40$
The perimeter is 40 cm.

10. $\frac{2}{3} = \frac{30}{45}$ $\frac{2}{3}$ of 45 m is 30 m.

(Suggested answers)

3	3	3	3	3	3	3	3	3	3

• ten 3-m pieces

4	4	4	3	3	3	3	3	3

• three 4-m pieces and six 3-m pieces

4	4	4	4	4	4	3	3

• six 4-m pieces and two 3-m pieces

11.

No. of Layers	No. of Cubes in Each Layer	No. of Cubes in Each Solid
1 ⎫+1 2 ⎬+1 3 ⎬+1 4 ⎭+1	1 2 × 2 = 4 3 × 3 = 9 4 × 4 = 16	1 × 1 = 1 4 × 2 = 8 9 × 3 = 27 16 × 4 = 64

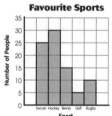

64 1-cm³ cubes are needed in the next solid.

12. (Suggested drawings)

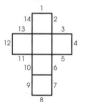 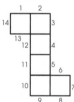

The net of a cube has a perimeter that is 14 times its side length.
Perimeter: $22 \text{ mm} \times 14 = 308 \text{ mm} = 30.8 \text{ cm}$
The perimeter of the net is 30.8 cm.

13.

Time (s)	Amount (g)
1	40 ⎫-5
2	35 ⎭
3	30
4	25
5	20
6	15
7	10
8	5
9	0

5 g of sand flows down the hourglass every second. It will take 9 seconds.

14.

Figure	Width (cm)	Length (cm)
1	1 ⎫+1	1 ⎫+2
2	2 ⎭	3 ⎭
3	3	5
4	4	7
5	5	9
6	6	11

Pattern rule: The width increases by 1 cm and the length increases by 2 cm each time.
Area of the 6th figure: $6 \times 11 = 66$
The area of the 6th figure is 66 cm².

15. 0.5 hour = 30 minutes
Practice in 21 days: $30 \times 21 = 630$
Florence practises the violin for 630 minutes in 21 days.

16. Side length of square: $784 \div 4 = 196$
Length of shaded part: $196 \div 2 = 98$
Width of shaded part: $196 \div 4 = 49$
Area of shaded part: $98 \times 49 = 4802$
The area of the shaded part is 4802 cm².

17. $2\frac{2}{3}$ hours = 2 hours 40 minutes
2 h 40 min before 6:37 p.m. = 3:57 p.m.
The time was 3:57 p.m. $2\frac{2}{3}$ hours ago.

18. $\frac{1}{4} = \frac{5}{20}$ $\frac{1}{4}$ of 20 is 5.
Perimeter: $5 + 1 + 5 + 1 = 12$
The perimeter of the rectangle is 12 cm.

19. The bars on the graph cover a total of 17 squares.
Equation: $17b = 85$
$b = 5$
The interval of the scale is 5.

Favourite Sports

20.

Day	No. of ⊘
1	4 ⎫+1
2	5 ⎭
3	7 ⎫+2
4	11 ⎫+4
5	19 ⎫+8
6	35 ⎫+16
7	67 ⎫+32

The increase doubles each day.
On the 7th day, the probability of picking a red marble is 3 out of 67.

Unit 3

1. 4709 ; 1245 ; 3464 ; 3464 ; 8 ; 433 ; 433 mL

2. C A S S I E
   $\frac{3}{6} = \frac{1}{2}$
   same as original
   $\frac{1}{2}$ of the letters in the mirror are the same as the original.

3.
   Length of frame: $32 + 1.5 + 1.5 = 35$
   Width of frame: $17 + 1.5 + 1.5 = 20$
   Area of picture: $32 \times 17 = 544$
   Area of picture and frame: $35 \times 20 = 700$
   Area of frame: $700 - 544 = 156$
   The area of the frame will be 156 cm².

ISBN: 978-1-77149-202-7

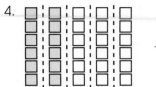

4.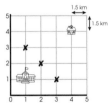

$\frac{2}{5}$ of 30 is 12.

No. of Earl Grey tea bags: $12 \times 58 = 696$
There are 696 Earl Grey tea bags in 58 packages.

5. A triangular pyramid has 4 triangles and a triangular prism has 2 triangles.
Triangular pyramid: $109 \times 4 = 436$
Triangular prism: $176 \times 2 = 352$
No. of triangles: $436 + 352 = 788$
788 wooden triangles are needed.

6.

Week	Gas Price (¢)
1	89.9
2	90.2
3	90.5
4	90.8
5	91.1

(+0.3)

The gas price increases by 0.3¢ each week.

The gas price in Week 5 will be 91.1¢.

7. Elapsed time: from 11:20 a.m. to 1:50 p.m.
= 2 h 30 min
Gas used for 2 hours: $50 \times 2 = 100$
Gas used for 30 minutes: $50 \div 2 = 25$
Total gas used: $100 + 25 = 125$
The helicopter used 125 L of gas for the flight.

8. Pop: 20
Country: 15
Jazz: 18
Rock: 7

$\frac{3}{4} = \frac{15}{20}$ ←pop (×5)

$\frac{3}{4}$ of 20 is 15.

Country music has $\frac{3}{4}$ of the number of votes for pop music. 15 children voted country music.

9. 6 km = 1.5 km + 1.5 km + 1.5 km + 1.5 km
6 km is 4 units on the map.
3 km = 1.5 km + 1.5 km
3 km is 2 units on the map.
Possible coordinates:
(1,3), (2,2), (3,1)
(Suggested answer)
One pair of possible coordinates for the library is (1,3).

10. Equation: $10w = 20$
$w = 2$
Length: $2 \times 4 = 8$ Area: $8 \times 2 = 16$
The area of the pool is 16 m².

11. Cost of remaining minutes:
$6.75 - $1.75 = $5 = 500¢
└ cost of first 5 minutes
No. of remaining minutes: 500¢ ÷ 50¢ = 10

Total minutes: $5 + 10 = 15$
Katie's phone call was 15 minutes long.

12. Groups of 3 chapters: $12 \div 3 = 4$
1 hour 15 minutes = 75 minutes
Total time: $75 \times 4 = 300$
It will take Candace 300 minutes to read the entire book.

13.

Row	No. of Quarters	No. of Nickels
1	1	2
2	2	3
3	3	4
4	4	5
5	5	6
6	6	7
7	7	8
8	8	9

Each row has 1 more quarter and nickel.
8 quarters: $2   9 nickels: $0.45
Row 8: $2 + $0.45 = $2.45
$2.45 in fewest coins:
1 toonie, 1 quarter, 2 dimes
Ali got 1 toonie, 1 quarter, and 2 dimes.

14. Stamp area:
$70 \times 50 = 3500$
Area from moving left: $80 \times 50 = 4000$
Area from moving up: $70 \times 50 = 3500$
Total area: $3500 + 4000 + 3500 = 11\,000$
The area of the shape created by the stamp is 11 000 mm².

15.

Day	Time
Mon	15 min 30 s
Tue	18 min 5 s
Wed	20 min 40 s
Thu	23 min 15 s
Fri	25 min 50 s

+2 min 35 s

Jeremy runs 2 min 35 s more each day.
On Friday, Jeremy will run for 25 min 50 s.

16.

Prism	No. of Vertices	No. of Sides on Its Base
Triangular	6	3
Rectangular	8	4
Pentagonal	10	5
Hexagonal	12	6
Heptagonal	14	7
Octagonal	16	8
Nonagonal	18	9

×2

The number of vertices in a prism is twice the number of sides its base has. A nonagonal prism has 18 vertices.

17. Rhombuses have 4 sides and triangles have 3 sides.
Sticks used for rhombuses : $4 \times 15 = 60$
Sticks used for triangles: $87 - 60 = 27$
Equation: $3s = 27$
$s = 9$
There were 9 triangles.

ISBN: 978-1-77149-202-7

Total no. of shapes: 9 + 15 = 24

Fraction of triangles: $\frac{9}{24} = \frac{3}{8}$

$\frac{3}{8}$ of the shapes were triangles.

18. Area of bulletin board: 60 × 60 = 3600

Area of poster: $\frac{1}{6} = \frac{600}{3600}$ $\frac{1}{6}$ of 3600 is 600.

(Suggested drawings)

Length: 60
Width: 60 ÷ 6 = 10
Dimensions:
60 cm by 10 cm

Length: 60 ÷ 2 = 30
Width: 60 ÷ 3 = 20
Dimensions:
30 cm by 20 cm

(Suggested answer)
The poster has an area of 600 cm² and dimensions of 30 cm by 20 cm.

19. Spinner A   Spinner B

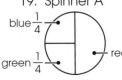 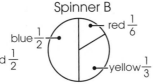

Blue: $\frac{1}{2} > \frac{1}{4}$

It will be more likely to spin blue on Spinner B. The probability is 1 out of 2.

20.

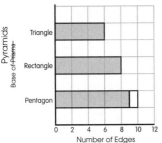

Edges
Number of ~~Vertices~~ in Pyramids

The title of the graph should be "Number of Edges in Pyramids". The label of the y-axis should be "Base of Pyramids". The bar for pentagon should show 10 edges instead of 9.

Unit 4

1. 442 ; 442 ; 558 ; 558 ; 2000
   $145 ; 20 ; $2900 ; $2900

2. Seats at square tables: 142 × 4 = 568
   Seats at pentagonal tables: 63 × 5 = 315
   Seats at hexagonal tables: 37 × 6 = 222
   Total seats: 568 + 315 + 222 = 1105
   The banquet hall can seat 1105 guests.

3. H O R I Z O N
   H O R I Z O N (rotated)
   6 letters are the same as the original. The probability that the rotated letter is the same as the original is 6 out of 7.

4. Fewest coins for $2.50: 2 loonies, 2 quarters
   Height: 1.9 + 1.9 + 1.6 + 1.6 = 7
   7 mm = 0.7 cm
   The shortest possible height is 0.7 cm.

5. Remaining sugar: 1 – 0.65 = 0.35
   $0.35 = \frac{35}{100} = \frac{7}{20}$
   $\frac{7}{20}$ cup of the sugar is left.

6. Total attendees: 1833 + 1167 = 3000
   $\frac{2}{5} = \frac{1200}{3000}$ $\frac{2}{5}$ of 3000 is 1200.
   Adults with jerseys: 1200 – 325 = 875
   875 adults wore jerseys.

7. Area of 1 tile: 8 × 6 = 48
   Area of countertop: 48 × 73 = 3504
   The area of the countertop is 3504 cm².

8. 20 quarters: $5
   Change: $5 – $4.85 = $0.15
   $0.15 in fewest coins: 1 nickel, 1 dime
   Leo will have 26 nickels and 36 dimes.

9. Units to the left:
   300 ÷ 100 = 3
   Units up:
   400 ÷ 100 = 4
   Units to the right:
   200 ÷ 100 = 2
   Units down:
   500 ÷ 100 = 5
   Yes, John is at the park now.

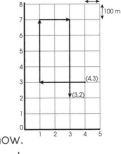

10.
Day	Quarters Earned	Nickels Earned	Money Earned ($)
Mon	1)+2	2)+2	0.35
Tue	3	4	0.95
Wed	5	6	1.55
Thu	7	8	2.15
Fri	9	10	2.75

She earns 2 more quarters and nickels each day.
Total: $1.75 + $0.35 + $0.95 + $1.55 + $2.15 + $2.75 = $9.50
Bethany will have $9.50 in total on Friday.

11. Groups of 8 pages: 104 ÷ 8 = 13
    No. of minutes: 15 × 13 = 195
    195 minutes = 3 hours 15 minutes
    3 hours 15 minutes after 9:30 a.m. is 12:45 p.m.
    Jordan will finish reading at 12:45 p.m.

12. Area of tile: 3 × 3 = 9
    No. of tiles: 5400 ÷ 9 = 600
    600 tiles are needed.

13.

Day	Pencil Length (cm)
March 13	18
March 16	16
March 19	14
March 22	12
March 25	10
March 28	8
March 31	6

+3 days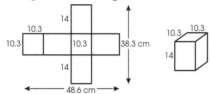

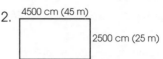

$\dfrac{1}{3}$ of 18 is 6.

The pencil will be $\dfrac{1}{3}$ of its original length on March 31.

14. Side length of square: $48.6 - 38.3 = 10.3$
2 lengths of rectangle: $38.3 - 10.3 = 28$
Length of rectangle: $28 \div 2 = 14$

Sylvester needs 12 sticks in total, with 8 sticks of 10.3 cm and 4 sticks of 14 cm.

15. Area of dough: $40 \times 40 = 1600$
Area of biscuit: $1600 \div 100 = 16$
$\dfrac{1}{4}$ of 16 is 4.
Area of biscuit after baking: $16 + 4 = 20$
The area of each baked biscuit is 20 cm².

16. 30 minutes = $\dfrac{1}{2}$ hour
Distance travelled: $216 \div 2 = 108$
Side length of triangle: $108 \div 3 = 36$
The length of one side of the triangle is 36 cm.

17. No. of students: $19 \times 11 = 209$
Students on each bus: $209 \div 5 = 41R4$
The remaining students each join one bus.
There will be 42, 42, 42, 42, and 41 students on the 5 buses.

18. Equation: $5t + 3t = 1568$
$t = 196$
No. of tickets: $196 + 196 = 392$
392 tickets were sold.

19.

Week	No. of Hours
1	1.5
2	2
3	2.5
4	3
5	3.5
6	4

+0.5

No. of hours increases by 0.5 each week.
Difference between Week 1 and Week 6:
4 hours – 1.5 hours = 2.5 hours = 150 minutes
Jimmy will exercise 150 minutes more in Week 6 than in Week 1.

20. No. of loonies: 5   No. of quarters: 20
No. of dimes: 50   No. of nickels: 100
No. of coins: $5 + 20 + 50 + 100 = 175$
The probability is 20 out of 175.

Unit 5

1. 1500 ; 1500 ; 1500 ; 1094 ; 406
406 baseball caps

2. 4500 cm (45 m)
2500 cm (25 m)
1 lap: $45 + 45 + 25 + 25 = 140$
2 laps: $140 \times 2 = 280$
Time: $280 \div 2 = 140$
It will take the train 140 s to travel 2 laps.

3. 20-point balls: $20 \times 15 = 300$
30-point balls: $30 \times 12 = 360$
40-point balls: $40 \times 0 = 0$
50-point balls: $50 \times 1 = 50$
Points from 10-point balls:
$730 - 300 - 360 - 0 - 50 = 20$
Equation: $10x = 20$
$x = 2$
Luke scored 2 10-point balls.

4. Side length of a small cube: $81 \div 3 = 27$
Area of 1 face of a small cube: $27 \times 27 = 729$
Having 1 face painted means having 729 cm² painted. So, 6 small cubes have 729 cm² painted.

5. Change: $2 - \$1.65 = \$0.35$
Possible combinations of $0.35:
- 7 nickels
- 5 nickels and 1 dime
- 3 nickels and 2 dimes
- 1 nickel and 3 dimes
- 1 quarter and 1 dime
- 1 quarter and 2 nickels
The probability of Jenny getting at least 1 dime is 4 out of 6.

6. 1.5 min = 1 min 30 s
$6\dfrac{4}{5}$ min = 6 min 48 s

$\dfrac{4}{5} = \dfrac{48}{60}$ (×12)

Total length before cutting:
1 min 30 s + 2 min 26 s + 6 min 48 s
= 10 min 44 s
126 s = 2 min 6 s
Length after cutting:
10 min 44 s – 2 min 6 s = 8 min 38 s
The final length of the video was 8 min 38 s.

7.
$\dfrac{1}{2}$ of the pizza has 4 slices.

Cost of 4 slices:
$3.80 + \$3.80 + \$3.80 + \$3.80 = \$15.20$
$\dfrac{1}{2}$ of the pizza costs $15.20.

ISBN: 978-1-77149-202-7

8. 5.4 5.4 6.7 __ __
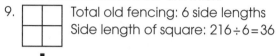

mode median

The fourth book must be 6.8 cm thick because it must be the smallest possible decimal that is greater than 6.7.

Thickest book:

$31.2 - 5.4 - 5.4 - 6.7 - 6.8 = 6.9$

The thickest book is 6.9 cm thick.

9.
Total old fencing: 6 side lengths
Side length of square: $216 \div 6 = 36$

Total new fencing: 7 side lengths
$= 36 \times 7$
$= 252$

Difference: $252 - 216 = 36$

36 m more fencing is needed.

10.

May 1 (Fri) (first Saturday)   May 2 (Sat)   May 9   May 16   May 23   May 30 (last Saturday)

There were 5 Saturdays in May.

Allowance each Saturday:

1 toonie: $2   3 dimes: $0.30

3 nickels: $0.15

Total: $2 + $0.30 + $0.15 = $2.45

Allowance in May:

$2.45 + $2.45 + $2.45 + $2.45 + $2.45 = $12.25

Lily received $12.25 in May.

11. $3\frac{1}{3}$ h = 3 h 20 min = 200 min

Carlos will play video games for 25 minutes on Thursday.

Day	Time (min)
Mon	200
Tue	100
Wed	50
Thu	25

(Mon 200, Tue 100 ÷ 2; ÷ 4)

12.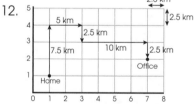

Distance travelled: $7.5 + 5 + 2.5 = 15$

Matt has travelled 15 km. He should travel 10 km to the right and 2.5 km down.

13. (Suggested answer)

No. of Adult Tickets	Money from Adult Tickets ($)	Money from Child Tickets ($)	No. of Child Tickets	Total No. of Tickets
96	672	1092−672=420	105	96+105=201
100	700	1092−700=392	98	100+98=198
104	728	1092−728=364	91	104+91=195

(×7; ÷4)

A total of 198 tickets were sold.

14. Tiles: 32 blue, 8 red, 40 green, 24 yellow, 16 black

No. of tiles: $32 + 8 + 40 + 24 + 16 = 120$

Area of 1 tile: $2 \times 3 = 6$

Area of mosaic: $6 \times 120 = 720$

The area of the mosaic was 720 cm².

15. Side length of square: $120 \div 4 = 30$

Area of mosaic: $30 \times 30 = 900$

Increase in area: $900 - 720 = 180$

No. of tiles added: $180 \div 6 = 30$

To have a mode of 16, 8 added tiles must be red.

Remaining yellow tiles: $30 - 8 = 22$

After adding:

red	black	blue	green	yellow
8+8=16	16	32	40	24+22=46

mode

The area of the mosaic is 900 cm².

22 yellow tiles were added.

16. No. of solids:
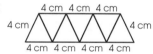

$3 + 2 + 2 + 4 + 1 = 12$

Only cubes and rectangular prisms have 8 vertices.

Cubes and rectangular prisms: $3 + 2 = 5$

The probability is 5 out of 12.

17. Perimeter:
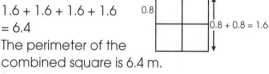

$1.6 + 1.6 + 1.6 + 1.6 = 6.4$

The perimeter of the combined square is 6.4 m.

18. Frame 7:

4 cm   4 cm   4 cm   4 cm   4 cm   4 cm   4 cm   4 cm   4 cm

Perimeter: $4 \times 9 = 36$

The perimeter of the shape is 36 cm.

19. The bed needs to be moved 2 units to the left and 3 units down.

2 units:

$0.5 + 0.5 = 1$

3 units:

$0.5 + 0.5 + 0.5 = 1.5$

Kevin should move his bed 1 m to the left and 1.5 m down.

$\frac{1}{4}$ counterclockwise   0.5 m

20. Area of tiling pattern: $92 \times 68 = 6256$

Two triangular prints make a square.

2 cm   2 cm   Area of square: $2 \times 2 = 4$

No. of squares: $6256 \div 4 = 1564$

No. of triangular prints: $1564 \times 2 = 3128$

There will be 3128 prints in the pattern.

Unit 6

1. Perimeter: $6.5 + 6.2 + 7.3 = 20$

20 m = 2000 cm

No. of flowers: $2000 \div 10 = 200$

There are 200 flowers.

ISBN: 978-1-77149-202-7

2.

Week	Cost ($)
1	1760 ⎞ −182
2	1578 ⎠
3	1396

Cost of 3 weeks:
$1760 + $1578 + $1396 = $4734
3 weeks at the ski lodge costs $4734.

3. Change: $10 − $6.70 = $3.30
$3.30 in fewest coins:
1 toonie, 1 loonie, 1 quarter, 1 nickel
The probability of picking a loonie is 1 out of 4.

4. Total time: 75 × 15 = 1125
1125 s = 18 min 45 s = $18\frac{3}{4}$ min
$18\frac{3}{4} > 18\frac{1}{2}$
Yes, it will take her longer than $18\frac{1}{2}$ minutes to put icing on 15 cookies.

5. 6 m = 600 cm
No. of tiles: 600 ÷ 10 = 60
There are 2 black tiles for every 3 tiles.
No. of sets of 3 tiles: 60 ÷ 3 = 20
No. of black tiles: 20 × 2 = 40
Mr. Matthews needs 40 black tiles.

6. $\frac{2}{3} \overset{×600}{=} \frac{1200}{1800}$ $\frac{2}{3}$ of 1800 is 1200.
×600

No. of bus wheels: 1800 − 1200 = 600
No. of buses: 600 ÷ 6 = 100
The factory will install wheels on 100 buses.

7. 2 toonies: $4
3 loonies: $3
6 quarters: $1.50
9 dimes: $0.90
8 nickels: $0.40
Total: $4 + $3 + $1.50 + $0.90 + $0.40 = $9.80
No, Melanie does not have enough money to buy a $10 book.

8. The bottom half is translated 1 unit to the right and 3 units down.
No. of side lengths in original shape: 18
No. of side lengths in new shape: 22
Difference in no. of side lengths: 22 − 18 = 4
Side length: 8 ÷ 4 = 2
Length of original shape: 2 × 5 = 10
Width of original shape: 2 × 4 = 8
Area of original shape: 10 × 8 = 80
The area of the original shape is 80 cm².

9. New TV: 93 × 52 = 4836
Old TV: 71 × 40 = 2840
Difference: 4836 − 2840 = 1996
The difference in area is 1996 cm².

10.

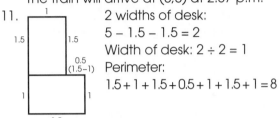

Time	Location
1:47	(10,15)
1:51	(8,12)
1:55	(6,9)
1:59	(4,6)
2:03	(2,3)
2:07	(0,0)

+4 min   −2 (10,15) ⎞ −3
        (8,12)

The train will arrive at (0,0) at 2:07 p.m.

11. 2 widths of desk:
5 − 1.5 − 1.5 = 2
Width of desk: 2 ÷ 2 = 1
Perimeter:
1.5 + 1 + 1.5 + 0.5 + 1 + 1.5 + 1 = 8
The perimeter of the desks is 8 m.

12.

Date	Time
Jan 2014	2 h 15 min
Jul 2014	1 h 55 min
Jan 2015	1 h 35 min
Jul 2015	1 h 15 min
Jan 2016	55 min
Jul 2016	35 min
Jan 2017	15 min ← less than $\frac{1}{2}$ hour

+6 months −20 min

Yes, the charging time would be less than $\frac{1}{2}$ hour in January 2017.

13. Area of a square unit: 3 × 3 = 9
Unit squares in the rectangle: 108 ÷ 9 = 12
Dimensions of a rectangle with 12 square units:
1 × 12 ⎤ too big for the grid
2 × 6 ⎦
3 × 4
(Suggested answer)
The coordinates of the other vertices are (2,6), (5,6), and (5,2).

14.

Month	Money Saved ($)
Jan	2 ⎞ +1
Feb	3 ⎞ +2
Mar	5 ⎞ +4
Apr	9 ⎞ +8
May	17 ⎞ +16
Jun	33 ⎞ +32
Jul	65 ⎞ +64
Aug	129

The increase in money saved is doubled each month.
Total amount:
$2 + $3 + $5 + $9 + $17 + $33 + $65 + $129 = $263
Change: $263 − $245.85 = $17.15
Yes, Ben will have enough money. His change will be $17.15.

15. The two shapes must be a square and a triangle.

The side length must be equal to the difference in their perimeters, or 18 cm.
Total perimeter: 18 × 7 = 126
The sum of their perimeters is 126 cm.

ISBN: 978-1-77149-202-7

16. No. of participants:
562 + 498 + 2146 + 1794 = 5000
No. of adults: 2146 + 1794 = 3940
The probability that the winner is an adult
is 3940 out of 5000.

17. Boxes soaked: $\dfrac{1}{10} \overset{\times 10}{\underset{\times 10}{=}} \dfrac{10}{100}$ $\dfrac{1}{10}$ of 100 is 10.

Boxes not soaked: 100 – 10 = 90
Books not soaked: 36 × 90 = 3240
3240 books were not soaked.

18. Equation: 7 × 8 × d = 728
56 × d = 728
d = 13
Whitney needs to work 13 days to afford
a $728 computer.

19. Triangular prism: 5 faces
Cube: 6 faces
Hexagonal pyramid: 7 faces
Faces: 5 5 5 6 ⑥ 7 7 7 7
The median number of faces is 6.

20. There are 4 numbers
greater than 500:
522, 692, 1044, 2088
The probability of rolling
a number greater than
500 is 4 out of 6.

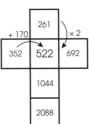

Unit 7

1. Possible combinations of 6 bills of $200:

$50	$50	$50	$20	$20	$10
$100	$20	$20	$20	$20	$20
$100	$50	$20	$20	$5	$5
$100	$50	$20	$10	$10	$10

The probability of picking a $100 bill is 3
out of 24.

2. Net: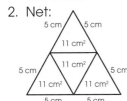
Side length of triangles:
15 ÷ 3 = 5
Perimeter of net:
5 × 6 = 30
Area of net:
11 × 4 = 44
The perimeter of the net is 30 cm and the
area of the net is 44 cm².

3. Boys with an A: $\dfrac{1}{4} \overset{\times 4}{\underset{\times 4}{=}} \dfrac{4}{16}$ $\dfrac{1}{4}$ of 16 is 4.

Girls with an A: $\dfrac{1}{2} \overset{\times 7}{\underset{\times 7}{=}} \dfrac{7}{14}$ $\dfrac{1}{2}$ of 14 is 7.

No. of students: 16 + 14 = 30
No. of students with an A: 4 + 7 = 11

No. of students without a A: 30 – 11 = 19
The probability of choosing a student who
did not get an A is 19 out of 30.

4. $0.8 = \dfrac{8}{10}$ $\dfrac{8}{10}$ of 10 km is 8 km.
Remaining km: 10 – 8 = 2
Remaining time: $\dfrac{5}{6} \overset{\times 10}{\underset{\times 10}{=}} \dfrac{50}{60}$ $\dfrac{5}{6}$ hour is 50 min.
60 – 50 = 10
No. of minutes for each km: 10 ÷ 2 = 5
Laura needs to run each remaining
kilometre in 5 minutes.

5. The number of minutes
increases by 5 and
then decreases by 3.

Day	No. of Minutes
Sun	21
Mon	26
Tue	23
Wed	28
Thu	25
Fri	30
Sat	27
Sun	32

Total no. of minutes:
26 + 23 + 28 + 25 + 30 + 27 + 32 = 191
3 hours = 180 minutes
Yes, Joshua will spend more than 3 hours
practising next week.

6. Times: 30.8 30.9 31.6 31.7 _____
fastest possible times with no mode
2 min 43 s = 163 s
Longest possible time:
163 – 30.8 – 30.9 – 31.6 – 31.7 = 38
Nicole's longest possible time was 38 s.

7. Length of track: 4.7 + 4.7 + 2.9 + 2.9 = 15.2
Length of 3 laps: 15.2 + 15.2 + 15.2 = 45.6
A race car will travel 45.6 km if it goes
around the track 3 times.

8. A triangular prism has 5 faces and has
3 sides in its base. It has 2 more faces
than sides.
Equation: $f - 2 = s$
faces sides
10 faces: 10 – 2 = s
8 = s
A shape with 8 sides is an octagon. The prism
that has 10 faces is an octagonal prism.

9. $2\dfrac{3}{4}$ h = 2 h 45 min $1\dfrac{5}{6}$ h = 1 h 50 min
Total time: 2 h 45 min + 1 h 50 min
= 4 h 35 min
It takes 4 hours and 35 minutes to upload
both files.

10.

Year	No. of Salmon
2016	10000
2015	8700
2014	7400
2013	6100
2012	4800
2011	3500

3500 salmon were released in 2011.

11. Red folders: $\dfrac{1}{5} \overset{\times 20}{=} \dfrac{20}{100}$ _{×20} $\dfrac{1}{5}$ of 100 is 20.

Blue and green folders: 100 − 20 = 80
Folders in 55 packages: 80 × 55 = 4400
There are 4400 blue and green folders in 55 packages.

12. (Suggested drawing)

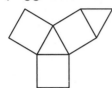

The side lengths of the squares and triangles must be the same.

The perimeter of the net is the sum of 10 side lengths.
Side length of squares: 180 ÷ 10 = 18
Area of square: 18 × 18 = 324
The area of one of the squares is 324 cm².

13. Students with brown hair:
$1 - 0.5 - 0.2 = 0.3 = \dfrac{3}{10}$
No. of students with brown hair:

$\dfrac{3}{10} \overset{\times 3}{=} \dfrac{9}{30}$ _{×3}   0.3 of 30 is 9.

The probability that the student has brown hair is 9 out of 30.

14. 2 hours = 120 minutes
5-minute intervals in 2 hours: 120 ÷ 5 = 24
No. of cups of latte: 13 × 24 = 312
The barista can make 312 cups of latte in 2 hours.

15.
Section	No. of People
1	1002
2	2013
3	3024
4	4035
5	5046

) +1011

Each section holds 1011 more people.
Total no. of people:
1002 + 2013 + 3024 + 4035 + 5046 = 15 120
The concert venue can hold 15 120 people in total.

16. Sliding to the left:
Area:
5.6 + 5.6 + 5.6 = 16.8

trapezoid

Sliding down:
Area of rectangle:
6 × 3 = 18
Total area: 5.6 + 18 = 23.6

pentagon

The shapes created are a trapezoid and a pentagon. The pentagon has a greater area.

17. Length of card: 450 mm ÷ 5 = 90 mm = 9 cm
Width of card: 350 mm ÷ 7 = 50 mm = 5 cm
Area of card: 9 × 5 = 45

No. of black cards: $\dfrac{3}{7} \overset{\times 5}{=} \dfrac{15}{35}$ _{×5} $\dfrac{3}{7}$ of 35 is 15.

Area of black cards: 45 × 15 = 675
The area of all the black cards is 675 cm².

18. Ottawa: 0.8 cm   Toronto: 0.5 cm
Difference: 0.8 − 0.5 = 0.3
Ottawa got 0.3 cm more precipitation than Toronto.

19.
Toronto	Sudbury	Hamilton	Ottawa
0.5	0.7	0.7	0.8

median and mode

Difference between Sudbury and Toronto:
0.7 − 0.5 = 0.2
Sudbury got 0.2 cm more precipitation than Toronto.

20. Capacity of auditorium: $\dfrac{2}{5} \overset{\times 1010}{=} \dfrac{2020}{5050}$ _{×1010}

The capacity of the auditorium is 5050.
Remaining capacity: 5050 − 2020 = 3030
The auditorium can hold 3030 more people.

Unit 8

1. Mark: $\dfrac{11}{10} = 1.1$
1.3 km > 1.1 km
Difference: 1.3 − 1.1 = 0.2
Kyle swims farther by 0.2 km.

2.
Hour	Hot Dogs Sold
1	2532
2	2878
3	3224

) −346

Hot dogs sold: 2532 + 2878 + 3224 = 8634
8634 hot dogs were sold in total.

3.
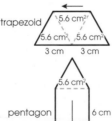

48 ÷ 8 = 6
32 ÷ 8 = 4
← crust

Area of each slice: 8 × 8 = 64
No. of slices: 6 × 4 = 24
There are 8 slices without crust.
$\dfrac{8}{24} = \dfrac{1}{3}$
Each slice is 64 cm². $\dfrac{1}{3}$ of the slices do not have any crust.

4. Charge from minutes: $10.35 − $2.85 = $7.50
$7.50 = 750¢ $0.75 = 75¢
No. of minutes: 750¢ ÷ 75¢ = 10
Michelle used the Internet for 10 minutes.

ISBN: 978-1-77149-202-7

5. White string: $\dfrac{3}{4} = \dfrac{18}{24}$ (×6) $\dfrac{3}{4}$ of 24 is 18.

   Red string: $1\dfrac{2}{3} = \dfrac{5}{3} = \dfrac{30}{18}$ (×6) $1\dfrac{2}{3}$ of 18 is 30.

   Total length: 24 + 18 + 30 = 72
   The total length of the 3 strings is 72 cm.

6.

Week	Sunrise Time
1	6:45 a.m.
2	6:51 a.m.
3	6:57 a.m.
4	7:03 a.m.
5	7:09 a.m.
6	7:15 a.m.

+6 min

Each week, the sunrise time is 6 minutes later.

7:15 a.m. is $\dfrac{1}{2}$ hour after 6:45 a.m. So, in Week 6, the sun will rise $\dfrac{1}{2}$ hour later than Week 1.

7. Divide the shape into 3 rectangles.
   Area of rectangle 1:
   20 × 5 = 100
   Area of rectangle 2:
   12 × 5 = 60
   Area of rectangle 3:
   20 × 5 = 100
   Total area:
   100 + 60 + 100 = 260
   The area of the shape is 260 cm².

8. Stephanie walked 3 units up and 2 units to the left to the park.

   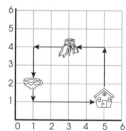

   No. of min to walk 1 unit: 6 ÷ 3 = 2

   Stephanie needs to walk 2 units to the left and 2 units down, and then 1 unit down and 4 units to the right.
   No. of units: 2 + 2 + 1 + 4 = 9
   No. of min: 9 × 2 = 18
   It takes Stephanie 18 min.

9. Perimeter of Field A:
   1784 + 1784 + 2412 + 2412 = 8392
   Perimeter of Field B: 8392 ÷ 2 = 4196
   2 widths of Field B: 4196 − 1492 − 1492 = 1212
   Width of Field B: 1212 ÷ 2 = 606
   The width of Field B is 606 m.

10. Area of front yard: 12 × 14 = 168
    No. of m² for $1: 168 ÷ 8 = 21
    Area of backyard: 21 × 10 = 210
    The area of Trevor's backyard is 210 m².

11.

Year	Cost of Token ($)
0	2.65
1	2.80
2	2.95
3	3.10
4	3.25
5	3.40

−0.15

Amount saved per token:
$3.40 − $2.65 = $0.75 = 75¢
Amount saved for 8 tokens:
75¢ × 8 = 600¢ = $6
Larry saved $6.

12. The shape is a square.
    Side length:
    96 ÷ 4 = 24
    Area of square:
    24 × 24 = 576
    The area of the shape is 576 cm².

    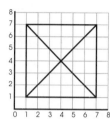

13. No. of red balls: $\dfrac{1}{4} = \dfrac{600}{2400}$ (×600) $\dfrac{1}{4}$ of 2400 is 600.

    No. of blue balls: 600 × 2 = 1200
    No. of green balls: 2400 − 600 − 1200 = 600
    No. of red or green balls: 600 + 600 = 1200
    The probability of picking a red or green ball is 1200 out of 2400.

14. No. of shots after 5:00: 25 + 50 = 75
    Donations after 5:00: 25¢ × 75 = 1875¢
    1875¢ = $18.75
    $18.75 in donations was made after 5:00.

15. Area of folded brochure: 621 ÷ 3 = 207
    Length of folded brochure: 207 ÷ 9 = 23
    Perimeter of folded brochure:
    23 + 23 + 9 + 9 = 64
    The perimeter of the folded brochure is 64 cm.

16. (6, 1) −3 (3, 5) +4
    Lucy walked 3 units to the left and 4 units up. She walked a total of 7 units.
    Distance of 1 unit: 1092 ÷ 7 = 156
    The distance of each unit of the grid is 156 cm.

17. Length of road marking and space:
    2.7 + 2.3 = 5
    1 km = 1000 m
    No. of white markings: 1000 ÷ 5 = 200
    A 1-km road has 200 white markings.

18. No. of boxes left: 4212 − 2011 = 2201
    No. of toys: 2201 × 10 = 22 010
    22 010 toys are left in the warehouse.

19. Length of 1 unit: 18 ÷ 6 = 3
    Perimeter of Room 1: 3 × 12 = 36
    Perimeter of Room 2: 3 × 8 = 24

Perimeter of Room 3: 3 × 10 = 30
Perimeter of Room 4: 3 × 12 = 36
Perimeter of Room 5: 3 × 10 = 30
Perimeters: 24 30 ③⓪ 36 36
The median perimeter of the rooms is 30 m.

20. 60 60 60 65 65 65 65 65 65 65
    65 65 65 70 ⑦⓪ 70 70 75 75 75
    75 75 75 75 80 80 80 80 80
Median: 70
No. of students: 3 + 10 + 4 + 7 + 5 = 29
No. of students with a mark higher than 70:
7 + 5 = 12
The probability of picking a student with a mark higher than the median is 12 out of 29.

Unit 9

1.
Day	No. of Shirts
1	7
2	20
3	33
4	46
5	59
6	72
7	85

)+13 Each day, 13 more shirts are given out.

Cost of shirts on 7th day: $25 × 85 = $2125
The cost of all the shirts given out on the 7th day is $2125.

2. 3 trays: $120
1 tray: $120 ÷ 3 = $40
10 lemon squares: $40
1 lemon square: $40 ÷ 10 = $4
Each lemon square costs $4.

15 cm
6 cm
10 squares in 1 tray

3. No. of 10 year olds: $\frac{1}{4} = \frac{2}{8}$ (×2) $\frac{1}{4}$ of 8 is 2.

No. of 11 year olds: $\frac{1}{2} = \frac{4}{8}$ (×4) $\frac{1}{2}$ of 8 is 4.

No. of 12 year olds: 8 − 2 − 4 = 2

Ages: 10 10 11 11 11 11 12 12
      mode ⌐────⌐───⌐⌐
           median

The median and mode ages are both 11 years old.

4. Jun: 600   Jul: 1100   Aug: 700
Total: 600 + 1100 + 700 = 2400
There were 2400 visitors.

5. Perimeter:
$w + w + 30 + 30 = 100$
$w + w + 60 = 100$
$w = 20$
Area: 30 × 20 = 600
The area of the rectangle is 600 cm².

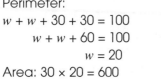
30
w   w
30

6. There are 30 days in June.

Days at cottage: $\frac{1}{5} = \frac{6}{30}$ (×6) $\frac{1}{5}$ of 30 is 6.

Days on a trip: $\frac{2}{3} = \frac{20}{30}$ (×10) $\frac{2}{3}$ of 30 is 20.

Days at home: 30 − 6 − 20 = 4
Travis spent 4 days at home.

7. A rectangular prism has 8 vertices and a square-based pyramid has 5 vertices.
Rectangular prisms: 8 × 160 = 1280
Square-based pyramids: 5 × 212 = 1060
No. of vertices: 1280 + 1060 = 2340
3 packs of modelling clay are needed.
Cost of modelling clay:
$35.50 + $35.50 + $35.50 = $106.50
The modelling clay costs $106.50.

8. Math notes: 1 − 0.5 − 0.1 = 0.4

Math notes: $0.4 = \frac{4}{10} = \frac{80}{200}$ (×20) 0.4 of 200 is 80.

The probability that it was a sheet of Math notes is 80 out of 200.

9. No. of dimes traded: 1020 − 409 = 611
Amount: 10¢ × 611 = 6110¢ = $61.10
$61.10 in fewest bills and coins:
1 $50 bill, 1 $10 bill, 1 loonie, 1 dime
Jerry did not get any $20 bills.

10. The bird flew 11 units in total.
Distance:
75 × 11 = 825

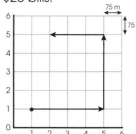
75 m
75 m

The bird flew 825 m.

11. Money from $12 books: $12 × 8 = $96
Money from $15 books: $15 × 5 = $75
Money from $18 books: $18 × 11 = $198
Money from $9 books:
$396 − $96 − $75 − $198 = $27
No. of $9 books sold:
$27 ÷ $9 = 3

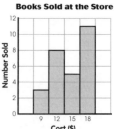
Books Sold at the Store
Number Sold
Cost ($)

3 $9 books were sold.

12. Money spent: $14.95 + $5 = $19.95
Total money before: $19.95 + $5.05 = $25

Money spent on snacks: $\frac{5}{25} = \frac{1}{5}$

Lily spent $\frac{1}{5}$ of her money on snacks.

ISBN: 978-1-77149-202-7

13. Perimeter of field: 62 + 62 + 43 + 43 = 210
    No. of seconds for Nicky: 210 ÷ 2 = 105
    No. of seconds for his dog: 210 ÷ 3 = 70
    Difference: 105 – 70 = 35
    It takes Nicky 35 seconds more to walk around the field than his dog.

14. Each day, she spends $15.24 more.

Day	Amount Spent ($)
Mon	23.54
Tue	38.78
Wed	54.02
Thu	69.26

    ⌉ +15.24

    Amount left:
    $1000 – $23.54 – $38.78 – $54.02 – $69.26
    = $814.40
    Isabel will have $814.40 left after Thursday.

15. No. of stamps: $\dfrac{1}{4} = \dfrac{30}{120}$ ← North America
    ×30 ×30

    Joey has 120 stamps in total.

    Europe: $\dfrac{1}{3} = \dfrac{40}{120}$ $\dfrac{1}{3}$ of 120 is 40.
    ×40 ×40

    Africa: $\dfrac{1}{6} = \dfrac{20}{120}$ $\dfrac{1}{6}$ of 120 is 20.
    ×20 ×20

    Asia: 120 – 30 – 40 – 20 = 30
    The probability of picking a stamp from Asia is 30 out of 120.

16. Length of Mr. Hamilton's classroom:

    $0.8 = \dfrac{8}{10} = \dfrac{24}{30}$ 0.8 of 30 is 24.
    ×3 ×3

    Width of Mr. Hamilton's classroom:

    $0.8 = \dfrac{8}{10} = \dfrac{16}{20}$ 0.8 of 20 is 16.
    ×2 ×2

    Area of Mr. Hamilton's classroom:
    24 × 16 = 384
    The area of Mr. Hamilton's classroom is 384 m².

17. Perimeter of 1 square: 15 × 4 = 60
    Perimeter of 15 squares: 60 × 15 = 900
    Perimeter of 1 triangle: 15 × 3 = 45
    Perimeter of 12 triangles: 45 × 12 = 540
    Total perimeter: 900 + 540 = 1440
    The total perimeter of the shapes is 1440 cm.

18. The tile is first reflected horizontally, and then rotated $\dfrac{1}{4}$ clockwise, and then translated 2 units to the left and 3 units down.

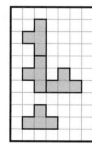

19. Length of 1 unit: 20 ÷ 10 = 2
    Area of 1 tile: 2 × 2 × 4 = 16
    Area of square: 16 × 4 = 64
    The area of the square is 64 cm².

20. Area to tile: 40 × 40 = 1600
    No. of tiles needed: 1600 ÷ 16 = 100
    Cost of tiles: 8¢ × 100 = 800¢ = $8
    $8 is needed to tile a 40 cm by 40 cm area.

Unit 10

1. Perimeter of park: 60 × 3 = 180
   No. of trees: 180 ÷ 3 = 60
   Time needed: 30 × 60 = 1800
   1800 min = 30 hours
   No. of 10-h durations: 30 ÷ 10 = 3
   Cost: $562.25 + $562.25 + $562.25 = $1686.75
   It will cost $1686.75 to plant all the trees.

2. Home runs of Team A:

   $\dfrac{2}{5} = \dfrac{400}{1000}$ $\dfrac{2}{5}$ of 1000 is 400.
   ×200 ×200

   Home runs of Team B:

   $\dfrac{1}{4} = \dfrac{250}{1000}$ $\dfrac{1}{4}$ of 1000 is 250.
   ×250 ×250

   Difference: 400 – 250 = 150
   Team A hit 150 more home runs.

3. No. of fish: 1354 + 2646 + 3000 = 7000
   No. of trout and salmon: 1354 + 2646 = 4000
   The probability that he will catch a trout or a salmon is 4000 out of 7000.

4. Time in one day: 24 × 2 = 48
   Time in one week: 48 × 5 = 240
   ↑
   School is from Monday to Friday.
   240 minutes = 4 hours
   Hannah spends 4 hours on the bus each week.

5. Difference in laps: 14 – 10 = 4
   Difference in distance: 100 × 4 = 400
   The difference is 400 m.

6. 1 km = 1000 m
   Median no. of laps: 1000 ÷ 100 = 10
   No. of laps:

Ben	Rosa	Ivy	Marc
6	10	10	14

   median

   Rosa must have swum 10 laps.
   Rosa swam 6 more laps.

ISBN: 978-1-77149-202-7

7.

No. of Strips	Perimeter (cm)
0	50+50+20+20=140 ⎫ −10
1	140−5−5=130 ⎭
2	120
3	110
4	100
5	90
6	80
7	70

Each strip cut decreases the perimeter by 10 cm.
The perimeter of the piece of paper after 7 strips are cut is 70 cm.

8. A cube has 6 identical faces.
Area of each face: 5400 ÷ 6 = 900
30 × 30 = 900 ← So, 30 cm is the side length.
The area of each face is 900 cm² and its side length is 30 cm.

9. Difference in 1 day: 7 − 3 = 4
There are 366 days in a leap year.
Difference in a leap year: 4 × 366 = 1464
The florist gives out 1464 more yellow flowers than red flowers in a leap year.

10. Yellow cards: 1 out of 5 from 50 is 10.
Blue and red cards: 50 − 10 = 40
Equation: $r + r + 12 = 40$
                   $r = 14$
Blue cards: 14 + 12 = 26
There are 10 yellow, 14 red, and 26 blue cards.

11. Time for a bracelet and a necklace:
12 + 10 = 22
Time for 11 sets: 22 × 11 = 242
242 min = 4 h 2 min
4 h 2 min after 9:24 a.m. is 1:26 p.m.
Pamela will finish at 1:26 p.m.

12. Movement after 1 dance move:
2 steps left + 1 step right → 1 step left
No. of steps to the left: 1 × 16 = 16
Distance: 25 × 16 = 400
Mike will be 400 cm to the left of his original position after 16 dance moves.

13. Ryan's money:
36 toonies: $72   14 dimes: $1.40
Total: $72 + $1.40 = $73.40
Taylor's money:
77 loonies: $77   17 quarters: $4.25
Total: $77 + $4.25 = $81.25
Taylor has more money.
No. of Ryan's bills: 36 + 14 = 50
No. of Taylor's bills: 77 + 17 = 94
Total no. of bills: 50 + 94 = 144
The probability that the bill belongs to the person who has more money is 94 out of 144.

14.

45 cm

A square has 4 lines of symmetry.
Perimeter: 45 × 4 = 180

James drew a square. Its perimeter was 180 cm.

15. Time left: 24 − 8.4 − 6.5 − 2.6 = 6.5
6.5 hours = 390 minutes
390 minutes are left in his day.

16. Times: 18   18   median = 31   44   100
               mode
31 × 2 = 62   180 − 18 − 18 − 44 = 100
62 − 18 = 44
3 hours = 180 minutes
The errands took 18 minutes, 18 minutes, 44 minutes, and 100 minutes.

17.

Week	Weight (kg)
1	3.5 ⎫ +0.2
2	3.7 ⎭
3	3.9
4	4.1
5	4.3
6	4.5
7	4.7
8	4.9

The baby gains 0.2 kg each week.
The baby's weight was 4.9 kg in Week 8.

18. Perimeter of each triangle: 180 ÷ 5 = 36
Side length: 36 ÷ 3 = 12
Perimeter of pentagon:
12 × 5 = 60 ← A pentagon has 5 sides.
The perimeter of the pentagon is 60 cm.

19. The probability of finding the treasure is 1 out of 49.
Possible locations:

The possible locations of the treasure are (1,6), (2,5), and (3,4).

20.

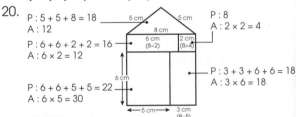

P : 5 + 5 + 8 = 18
A : 12
P : 6 + 6 + 2 + 2 = 16
A : 6 × 2 = 12
P : 6 + 6 + 5 + 5 = 22
A : 6 × 5 = 30
5 cm   5 cm
8 cm
6 cm (8−2)   2 cm (8+4)
6 cm
P : 8
A : 2 × 2 = 4
P : 3 + 3 + 6 + 6 = 18
A : 3 × 6 = 18
5 cm   3 cm (8−5)

Side length of small square: 8 ÷ 4 = 2
Perimeter greater than 16 cm: 3 out of 5
Area less than 12 cm²: 1 out of 5
It is more likely that the missing shape has a perimeter greater than 16 cm.

ISBN: 978-1-77149-202-7